BE CLEAR

HOW TO COMMUNICATE

SUCCESSFULLY

be clear – how to communicate successfully

Stanley's Books Ltd

Published by Stanley's Books Ltd, 8 Princess Road West, Leicester LE1 6TP

Tel/Fax 0845 456 7094

Editor: Jo Parfitt

Editorial contributions: Ingrid St Clare, Mike Edwards, Claire Biggadyke

Illustrations: Robert Bain

Photograph: Stu Williamson Photography

Design: Stuart Keil

ISBN-10: 0-9551614-1-X
ISBN-13: 978-0-9551614-1-4

BE CLEAR

HOW TO COMMUNICATE

SUCCESSFULLY

CHRISTINE SEARANCKE

DEDICATION

To John Paddick and Jonathan Flowers for starting me on the journey.

To Paul, Mark and the Company Secretary for gin, counselling and sustenance along the way.

CONTENTS

FOREWORD BY ROBERT CRAVEN

Most people hate standing up and giving a presentation. That's why a simple, practical book on the subject is needed.

My public speaking puts me in front of over 5,000 business people a year and I wish that such a book existed when I started out but nothing like it existed then. I had to learn the hard way!

Christine was the perfect person to write this book. Her knowledge and experience of the subject has been combined with her ability to put across her ideas in a digestible form. The result is a book that will be read by first-time speakers as much as by the 'old hands'.

Public speaking can be the most exhilarating thing to do - to see that people are listening to your every word... to see that you are communicating... is a great feeling. Follow Christine's advice and you too will enjoy your presentations as you see your audiences understanding and responding to what it is that you are putting across.

We are all measured by how well we present... so a book that helps you make better presentations will help you to sell yourself as well as your ideas. This book could seriously make you more successful!

Go For It!

Robert Craven

Keynote Speaker and Author of *Kick-Start Your Business* and *Customer Is King*

INTRODUCTION

Communicating is a skill that we all use every day. We give information, sell ideas, ask for assistance and motivate those around us. This book is about how to communicate better in any situation, particularly business situations and most particularly when preparing a specific presentation or document.

Some people are seen as natural-born communicators. They are the people who seem to get their message across clearly and effortlessly. In addition, they always seem to get people to agree to whatever they want and inspire people to follow them no matter what dangers they will face in so-doing. I do not believe that good communicators are *born* like that. I believe that they are *made*. In reality these people have usually learned the tools and techniques of good communication, whether they have done this consciously or by subconsciously imitating others.

Few of us are taught how to communicate – yet most senior business and professional people spend the majority of their time doing just that. Were I to ask you right now what training you have had to help you choose what information to put into a document, or how to prepare the content of a presentation or workshop, you would probably tell me that you have not had any. The look on your face would suggest that you have also never thought of having any.

This book is a step-by-step guide that tells you how to prepare clear and concise communication for any situation. It is not about theory. It is about being practical and hands-on. It provides simple steps that you can put into practice from the moment you read them.

By the time you reach the end of this book you will know what content to include for any piece of communication. You will know the best order to put it in based on clear objectives and thorough research of your audience. You will learn a process that can be applied whenever you are communicating with a specific audience at a particular time. I call this Single Point Communication. This might be an email or a telephone call, or it could be a meeting, a formal presentation or a lengthy document. The key thing is that if the audience or the time changes, so will what you say and how you put it together.

The chapters in the book focus on each of the stages of the **Be Clear Seven Stage Process**™ that I use whenever I am working with a client. The process can be applied to both written and verbal communication. This book focuses on presenting information *verbally* as I have found that this is the area about which most people seek my advice. As a result, the examples I draw on tend to be one-to-one sales meetings, competitive tender presentations (also known affectionately as 'beauty parades'), seminars, webinars and conference presentations.

The tools and techniques defined in this book are simple and easy to use, so with a little application they will quickly become an automatic part of your preparation for any communication.

How will you get the most from this book?

In order to get the most from this book, I recommend that you set aside half an hour each day for a week. During that half hour you will have time to read one of the chapters and try out the tool that is explained there.

If you have a meeting or presentation coming up in a few weeks try applying each of the stages to that piece of communication. Once you have read the whole book, you will have a good understanding of how all the stages build together and will then be able to begin your preparation in earnest.

For some people, this will sound far too methodical and much too much like hard work. If you are one of those people who likes to work from a broad overview and dip in and out of chapters, then the key sections for you are likely to be Chapters 1, 5 and 6, though of course I advise you to study them all.

Within each chapter you will find a step-by-step guide to that stage of the process, a summary of how to make that stage work for you and some short cuts for when time is really short.

There are also three case studies, which run throughout the book. You can follow the characters of Boffin the Inventor, Peter the Project Manager and Chrystal and Christof the Creativity Consultants to see how their ideas change as they go through each stage of the process. Similarities between these characters as well as other examples in the book, and anyone in real life is entirely coincidental!

A word of warning

Just before you read on to discover how to be a great communicator, a word about two things this book does *not* do for you.

1 – It doesn't tell you how to design great PowerPoint slides or cobble together two or three old presentations so the audience cannot see the join. Mainly because you can't do this and get away with it.

2 – It doesn't mean that you will finish your presentation on a fantastic adrenalin-fueled high. Mainly because you will be so well prepared that you won't need all that adrenalin. The high will come from knowing that you have actually **achieved your objectives, by delivering a clear message**.

What this book
helps with

This book will help you to excel at Single Point Communication, that is communicating with a specific audience at a particular time, including:

- Bidding for competitive tenders
- Running workshops
- Phone calls
- Conference speeches
- Seminars
- Performance reviews
- Hosting meetings
- Documents
- Emails
- Funding bids
- Webinars
- Project updates
- Team meetings
- Presenting ideas
- Sales pitches
- Beauty parades
- Letters
- Proposals
- Positive use of any 'face-to-face' time

Case studies

Three case studies run throughout the book. The three case studies are:

- Boffin the Inventor, speaking at a conference about his new invention the Turbo Powered Wimbley Stick.
- Peter the Project Manager, preparing for his monthly update meeting with his boss Sarah.
- Chrystal and Christof the Creativity Consultants, who are preparing for the final presentation in a competitive tender.

This is their situation before they begin to use the **Be Clear Seven Stage Process**™.

Boffin the Inventor

Boffin is a highly intelligent man, some might say that he has a brain the size of a small planet. Over the years he has invented many things, his most recent brainchild is the Turbo Powered Wimbley Stick.

Having spent years developing this revolutionary product, Boffin is now ready to sell his marvelous invention. There are many potential uses in the automotive industry and this is where he is targeting his activity.

A Public Relations (PR) company is working with Boffin to raise industry awareness of his revolutionary tool. He is delighted that the PR Company has secured him a speaking slot at a major automotive industry conference. It is a real coup for him. He has never addressed an industry conference before . . . but he supposes it will be much like lecturing an audience of undergraduates! I wonder whether he has this right?

Boffin is looking forward to telling the conference delegates all about his invention and in particular talking about *all* the challenges he has had to overcome in the seven years since he first had the idea. He thinks that people are bound to buy his invention when they know how much time and effort went into it.

The conference is about six weeks away and Boffin has been telling his friend Igor how difficult it is going to be to fit all his information into a 40-minute speaking slot. Hearing this, Igor suggests that he follows the **Be Clear Seven Stage Process™**.

Peter the Project Manager

Peter is really hardworking, conscientious and reliable; he could be called a prince among project managers. He thoroughly enjoys his job except for one thing – his monthly update meeting with his boss Sarah!

Every month, Peter spends hours and sometimes days preparing for their meeting. Every month, he ends up frustrated and disappointed with the outcome of the meeting. Sarah always goes off at tangents so that he doesn't have time to tell her a lot of the information that he is sure she needs to know.

After the most recent meeting he said to his partner, Chris: "I don't know how Sarah manages to run our department, half the information I prepare for her she doesn't seem to want to hear. It's all really important stuff. If I was doing her job I'm sure that I would want to know it all, and probably much more besides."

At this point Chris suggested that he try the **Be Clear Seven Stage Process**™ for his meeting preparation. Peter didn't really see how he could prepare any differently. But, he agreed to try if only in the hope of finding a way to keep Sarah quiet so that he could tell her all she needed to know!

Chrystal and Christof the Creativity Consultants

Chrystal and Christof are the founders and owners of a fast growing professional consultancy specialising in helping people to be more creative. They work well together complementing each others skills, but sometimes Christof has to curtail some of Chrystal's wilder ideas in the name of commerciality. They have been in business for four years.

At present, they are competing for a major new contract, which could double the size of their business. It is a competitive tender issued by a government department. Both Chrystal and Christof have been in discussion with the department for some months and have already submitted a response to an Invitation to Tender (ITT). Their response ran to over 100 pages.

Very soon they will have the final meeting with the panel responsible for awarding the contract. Over the years Chrystal and Christof have attended several meetings like this. Many readers will know this type of meeting as a 'beauty parade'.

Both Chrystal and Christof are concerned that whilst they are usually short listed, they often fail to win the business. From recent feedback they believe that it is their presentation at the beauty parade that is letting them down. This is really annoying because they know that their consultancy is far better than the competition. As a result they have both been working particularly hard over the last few weeks on their final presentations.

This meeting will last two hours and they have decided that each of them should present for 45 minutes leaving a full 30 minutes at the end for questions. As always, Chrystal who is Head of Creativity, will present about the expertise that they bring; whilst Christof will talk about how the project will be run, the team they will use and all the practical management aspects, as he is Head of Operations.

A couple of weeks ago they took on Mike as their tenth member of staff. He is their first dedicated Business Development Manager. Until now Chrystal and Christof have done this between them. As this is such a major contract they decide to spend an afternoon with Mike going through their final presentations. Chrystal said: "After all we have employed him as a professional to go out and get new business, so let's see if he can suggest any ways that we can improve our approach."

Mike is immediately concerned when he realises that this is the first time Chrystal and Christof have seen the content of each other's presentations . . . even if they think it will appear seamless because they have used the same PowerPoint template! A very quick review of the content shows how disjointed the whole thing will appear to an external audience. So given that they have the afternoon and a couple of days before the beauty parade, Mike decides that he will quickly take them through the **Be Clear Seven Stage Process**™ with the aim of giving them a more coherent message.

BE CLEAR SEVEN STAGE PROCESS™

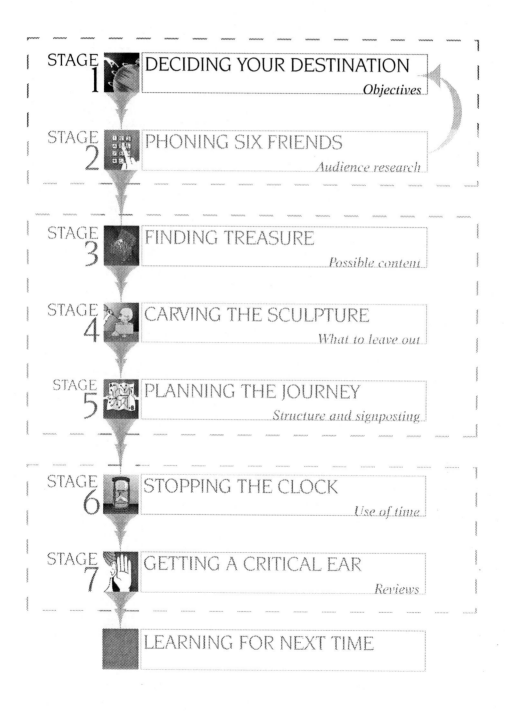

STAGE 1	DECIDING YOUR DESTINATION	*Objectives*
STAGE 2	PHONING SIX FRIENDS	*Audience research*
STAGE 3	FINDING TREASURE	*Possible content*
STAGE 4	CARVING THE SCULPTURE	*What to leave out*
STAGE 5	PLANNING THE JOURNEY	*Structure and signposting*
STAGE 6	STOPPING THE CLOCK	*Use of time*
STAGE 7	GETTING A CRITICAL EAR	*Reviews*
	LEARNING FOR NEXT TIME	

– 1 –

DECIDING YOUR DESTINATION In this
chapter we explore the foundation of all good communication –
clear, concise and measurable objectives.

Stage 1

This first stage appears so simple it could easily be overlooked. It will show you how to set clear objectives for a specific meeting or presentation. Read on to learn how to use a tool that will help you to be more precise about your objectives. When combined with Stage 2 it is a powerful tool that helps you to see your message not from your own perspective, but from the audience's.

Stage 1 will help you to answer the following important question:

'Where do you want to take the audience?'

You have the ability to guide your audience to wherever you want them to be. The important thing is that you need to be really clear about where that is. You must decide the end point, or final destination, right at the beginning of your preparation. Once you have made that decision, the remaining stages in the process are about the route you take to get there, as well as the way in which you take your audience to that particular destination.

Fortunately, I rarely work with a client who doesn't have an objective. I expect you have one too, so that's a good start. But equally, it is rare that I work with clients who have spent enough quality thinking time considering their objectives for a specific audience, at a particular time. The more time you spend considering your objectives, writing them down and discussing them, the more likely you are to succeed with your communication.

If you think that you always have clear objectives for your presentation, take a moment to consider the following questions:

*1 –   Have you ever been in a meeting, workshop or presentation
where someone was putting forward information to you and at
the end of it you asked yourself: 'what was all that about?'*

If like most people, you can say that you have been in that
situation, consider the next question:

*2 –   How do you know that **your objectives** are always really
clear?*

Most people have neither a clearly defined process for setting
their communication objectives, nor a robust method of
checking whether or not they achieved them. By the end of
this chapter you will have a tool that enables you to do both.
It is a tool that I use all the time and I find my clients using
again and again.

Now you might be wondering how long such a great tool is
going to take you to learn and more importantly how long it
will take to implement. Well, you will be pleased to know that
once you have read this chapter you will immediately be able
to start applying it to all of your Single Point Communication.
Whether you spend five minutes or five hours on this stage
will depend on your audience and the importance of the
presentation or meeting.

The more time you spend on Stage 1:

• The easier the rest of the process will be
• The clearer your presentation will be
• The more effective the outcome will be

Why 'deciding your destination' really matters

"If you don't know where you are going, every road will get you nowhere." (Henry Kissinger)

Clear objectives are the foundation of every aspect of successful business practice. This applies as much to a specific presentation or meeting as it does to a five-year corporate strategy.

When you are in a meeting or giving a presentation your aim is to move the audience from where they are now to where you want them to be. This doesn't mean you will move them physically, but it does mean you will move them mentally and emotionally. For example, at the end of your presentation you might want them to have:

- A greater knowledge of your subject
- A deeper understanding
- An awareness of opportunities
- An appreciation of the impact on their own work
- An openness to talk to you
- A desire to buy your product

The possibilities are endless.

Without clear objectives there is always huge potential for leaving your audience feeling confused, remembering only the unimportant facts, or at the very worst, thinking that you haven't considered their needs.

If you have no reason or purpose for moving the audience in some way, why waste everyone's time including your own having a meeting just for the sake of it? Cancel the meeting until you have something to say!

Assuming that you do want to move the audience in some way, then you need to be absolutely clear about your objectives.

Stage 1 is vital because it helps you decide:

- What information to include
- What information to leave out
- What is the best order for your information

The tool – deciding your destination

Used correctly and in conjunction with Stage 2, this tool is simple, constructive and highly effective. It is, however, rarely easy.

Six steps to the right destination

If possible work with one or two other people and go through the following six steps to help you decide your objectives. In an ideal world work face-to-face, but if this is not possible you can work with them by telephone or email. The important thing is to get someone else's input.

*1 – **Ask yourself...** "What do I want the audience to **do** (or **do** differently) at the end of my presentation?"*

- Write down all the answers that you come up with. Using moveable notes such as Post-it® notes is ideal as you will often want to move ideas from one part of this step to another.

- Review them to find the one or possibly two things that you really need the audience to **do**.
- Notice that the other things will usually be actions that flow from achieving the primary objective.

2 – **Ask yourself...** *"What does the audience need to **think**, in order to do what I need them to do?"*

- The key word here is **think**, by which I mean what are the cognitive, rational, logical thoughts your audience needs to have in order to move to the place you want them to be.
- Remember these are the things the audience will need to **think**, not the things **you** would need to **think**.
- Brainstorm as many things as you can here. Again use Post-it® notes or something similar if possible.

3 – **Ask yourself...** *"What does the audience need to **feel** in order to do what I need them to do?"*

- Write down the feelings or emotions that you believe your audience needs to experience in order to move to the place you want them to be.
- Examples are 'the audience needs to feel excited, or comfortable, or threatened, or inspired'.
- Most business people find this step a bit of a challenge. This is because we don't tend to think about feelings or emotion very much, although our rational mind can tell us that most advertising is based on emotion and the majority of decisions are more emotionally driven than rationally driven. I look more at feelings a little later in this chapter.

4 – **Ask yourself...** *"What will the audience **say** if they are going to do what I need them to do?"*

- If you know your audience very well, for example if you are presenting to your boss, then you will be able to put down exactly the sort of words they will use. For example, 'fantastic, get on to it right away and let me know if you need anyone blasting out of the way!' Or 'this is all very well (heavy sigh) but you'll need to get George on your side and that won't be easy (another heavy sigh)'.

- You might also include questions that you expect the audience will ask if they are making the links in their own mind that you want them to make.

- If you are speaking at a seminar or conference, imagine what things the audience should **say** to you after your speech, perhaps during lunch or a coffee break.

5 – *Review Steps 2 to 4 and refine them*

Now is the time to prioritise and consider the key things that the audience will need to **think, feel** and **say** if they are to do what you need them to **do**. Whilst there are no specific rules here, aim for the following:

- Reduce the number of **thinks** to four or five
- Reduce the number of **feels** to one or two
- Reduce the number of **says** to two or three

If you have more you will be trying to move your audience too far in one meeting or presentation. Be realistic and move something into your plan for another meeting or document if you are trying to achieve too much.

6 – *Check for congruence*

All the things that you need the audience to **think, feel** and **say** must build towards what you want them to **do**. There can be no conflict between one and another. For example, if you need the audience to **think** 'this person will be safe and reliable' there could be a conflict if you wanted them to **feel** 'excited'. The corresponding feelings for safe and reliable would usually be comfortable, confident or secure.

The key thing here is to consider the different options and to decide what is best for this particular audience at this specific time. Resolving any conflict in your objectives now will help you to design a better piece of communication and will help your audience when they are listening to you.

Design Principles Template – objectives

By now you will have a clearly defined set of objectives. These will form a vital part of your preparation. You will need to refer back to them constantly so I suggest that you record them in the Design Principles Template. A blank copy is shown on the next page and a copy can be downloaded from http://www.beclear.co.uk/hints.htm.

The Design Principles Template is a very simple way to record your objectives for the presentation.

The Design Principles provide:

- A check point throughout the preparation of your presentation
- A clear statement of your objectives for anyone who is involved in reviewing your presentation
- A starting point for your post-presentation or meeting review

Design Principles Template – objectives

Presentation to / meeting with _____ **in** _____, _____	

At the end of the _____ I want the audience to:

DO	• • •

In order to do this, _____ needs to:

THINK	• • • • •

In order to do this, _____ needs to:

FEEL	• • • • •

If _____ is going to do what I want, they will:

SAY	• • • • •

How feelings make a difference

This book is all about the content of your communication, rather than the delivery. However, to really understand the importance of feelings for the design of your presentation try the following exercise – it's the only one in the book!

The exercise

Find a friend or colleague to work with then tell them about your journey to work today. You should aim to tell them everything of importance in less than a minute. Your objective is to make them **think** 'I am informed about their journey.' Once you have done that ask the other person to tell you about their journey, again with the objective of informing you about the journey.

Now repeat the exercise but this time the objective is for the listener to **feel** 'inspired' about the speaker's journey.

You will soon see how the story of the journey changes. I recommend that you make time to try this exercise today as it only takes a few minutes and the results can be remarkable. If you prefer not to, have a look at Appendix 1 to see the words that I might use for the same journey but with different objectives. You won't be able to experience the change in body language or tonality but it should give you an idea of the differences in pure content and the way descriptive words can be used.

It is incredibly important to consider feelings as part of your objectives. Just think how much easier it is to get your message across to an audience that feels intrigued to learn more, as opposed to an audience that feels bored.

A list of some common emotions that you might want the audience to **feel** are shown in Appendix 2.

If you would like to, you can carry on the exercise using other emotions – for example try happy, miserable or scared. It's fun honest!

Examples

Working with your co-presenters

"But Christine, you've been writing presentations for us for so long, you know what's going on. Just start writing the presentation . . . "

This is what my client David said at a time when I was working with him and his team on a regular basis.

He was correct in saying that I knew a lot about what was going on, but I didn't know his objectives for this very important presentation to the Group CEO. Worse still I didn't know if he had discussed the objectives with his two co-presenters so I politely declined to write anything until all four of us had met to agree the objectives.

The next day, over a cup of coffee with David the Managing Director (MD) of the business, Sonia the Sales Director and Tom, the Product Development Director, the scene was something like this . . .

"So what do we need the Group CEO to do?" I asked Sonia.

"We need him to recognise how important it is that we have more sales people to get out and sell our existing products," she replied.

I turned to Tom and asked whether he agreed.

"Absolutely not!" he replied. "There's no point having more sales people until we've a broader range of products. He needs to recognise the importance of funding more product development."

At this point David intervened. "Don't you two realise that the most important message for all of us at the moment, is that if the Board decide to close this division they recognise what a great team of people we have, so that they get the chance of jobs in other parts of the business."

As you can see, three people had three very different objectives. None of them could be called 'wrong'. The Sales Director was focused on sales and the Product Development Director was passionate about products whilst the MD was thinking about the threat of closure. However, the potential for mixed messages and focusing on the wrong aspects was enormous.

Once the differences were known and the whole group could see the bigger picture, it was quite easy for the directors to discuss their views and see that the MD was absolutely right. They then agreed a clearly defined set of objectives focused on showing what a great team of people they had and gave me a good brief about the key messages to be included.

Key point

If you are:

- Presenting with other people
- Writing a presentation for someone else
- Contributing to someone else's material

The first and most important thing you should do is to get everyone together to discuss and agree the objectives.

Make it relevant

'Why did Lynn keep telling me things about the XYZ Group that were important to her, instead of things that were important to me?' I asked myself.

This thought occurred to me after two different people had told me about the same organisation, but in very different ways.

The first person to tell me about the XYZ Group was Lynn. For the previous 12 months and probably longer, she had told me how it would support me as an independent consultant. In my mind, I wasn't an independent consultant and I didn't need that kind of support, so I had never really listened to anything Lynn said.

When Nicola told me about the organisation, she talked about how it helped growing businesses with their sales and marketing. In my view I had a growing business and was interested in innovative sales and marketing techniques, so I was very interested.

You see, Lynn had told me the things that were important to **her**. Whilst, Nicola had told me the things that she thought would be important to **me** – and she was right!

Key point

Focus on what is important to the particular audience you are speaking to, even if this is entirely unimportant to you.

Making 'deciding your destination' work for you

In summary, the key things to remember about Stage 1 are:

- **Write your objectives down** – until you write them down they will be a rather nebulous, unspecific cloud floating somewhere in your head. Once they are on paper they become firmer and it is easier to spot if they conflict in any way.

- **Get someone else to do it with you** – if this isn't possible get an external view after Stages 1 and 2.

- **Work through the questions in the way that is easiest for you** – some people find it easier to start with **think** or **feel**, rather than **do**.

- **Be realistic about what you can expect to achieve in the timescale** – trying to take your audience too far, too fast increases the chance of losing their interest and attention.

- **Agree the objectives with sponsors and co-presenters** – if you are presenting with other people or if you are contributing to someone else's presentation or meeting always agree the objectives with them at the outset.

Above all, remember to consider the outcomes from the audience's perspective, so the more audience research you do the better!

No time for 'deciding your destination'

When time is precious, as it usually is, deciding your destination is time well spent, not time wasted.

The most common thing people say to me is: "I didn't think I had time for the objectives stage, I thought I knew what I wanted to achieve, but then I got in a real mess and couldn't figure out what to include or what to leave out . . . so eventually, I decided it might help to think a bit about the objectives . . . suddenly it all fell into place. I'll always do it at the outset from now on, no matter how little time I have!"

This stage can take five minutes or five hours, it depends on the importance of the presentation or meeting and the complexity of the messages you have to get across.

Finding time for 'deciding your destination' will enable you to:

- Establish clearly where you want to take the audience
- Check whether you succeeded
- Receive really constructive feedback from your reviewers

What next?

Move on to Chapter 2 – *phoning six friends*. Chapter 2 will help you to know who your audience are, to do a bit of valuable research and to find out more about them. Using these two chapters together will help you to focus on what the audience needs to hear. This is the opposite of what happens so often in presentations where you end up listening to what the presenter wants to tell the audience.

At the end of Chapter 2 you will know so much more about your audience that it makes sense to go back and revisit your objectives, as covered here. Going from Stage 1, to Stage 2 and then back, to Stage 1 again will become a positive cycle on which you can build firm foundations for your presentation or meeting.

CASE STUDIES – STAGE 1

Boffin the Inventor

Boffin worked through the first stage of the process with his friend Igor. Whilst Igor is also an inventor he has had more commercial success with his inventions than Boffin and he persuaded him that people would be more interested in what the product would do for them, rather than the time and trouble that had gone into the design phase.

After they had completed Stage 1 and 2 they filled in the Design Principles Template:

Presentation to the Automotive Industry Conference in Japan, May 20xx

At the end of the conference presentation I want the audience to:	
DO	• Approach me and ask for more information about the Turbo Powered Wimbley Stick

In order to do this, the audience needs to:	
THINK	• This Wimbley Stick could help streamline our process quite significantly • That using this instead of our existing solution would be a big cost saving • We might gain a competitive advantage if we had sole rights • Being involved at the outset might mean we can influence future enhancements

In order to do this, the audience needs to:	
FEEL	• Excited

If the audience is going to do what I want, they will:	
SAY	• What a really great idea! • I want to talk to him now – before my competitors do

Peter the Project Manager

Peter worked with his partner Chris to decide on the objectives for the next meeting with his boss Sarah.

When they had finished Stage 1 they completed the Design Principles Template:

Update meeting with Sarah, April 20xx

	At the end of the meeting I want Sarah to:
DO	• Agree the course of action that I am pursuing • Leave me to get on with it

	In order to do this, Sarah needs to:
THINK	• Peter has everything well under control • He has taken all the right actions to mitigate possible risks • He is involving all the right people to make this happen

	In order to do this, Sarah needs to:
FEEL	• Confident

	If Sarah is going to do what I want, she will:
SAY	• Thanks Peter that's all I need to know • You've obviously got everything well under control

Chrystal and Christof the Creativity Consultants

Chrystal and Christof allowed Mike to facilitate a full and frank discussion about what were the most important points to get across to the audience at this crucial meeting. They both had quite different views but had assumed the other person thought as they did.

Eventually they came to an agreement and then refined the objectives to the following in the Design Principles Template:

Final presentation to the Board responsible for the Creativity Programme, March 20xx

At the end of the meeting we want the Board to:	
DO	• Award us the contract

In order to do this, the Board needs to:	
THINK	• These people really understand our issues • They are the low risk option • Their approach is really flexible • They will work with us to make the project a long-term success

In order to do this, the Board needs to:	
FEEL	• Comfortable

If the Board is going to do what we want, they will:	
SAY	• How soon can you start? • What else can we do to help make this a real success?

BE CLEAR SEVEN STAGE PROCESS™

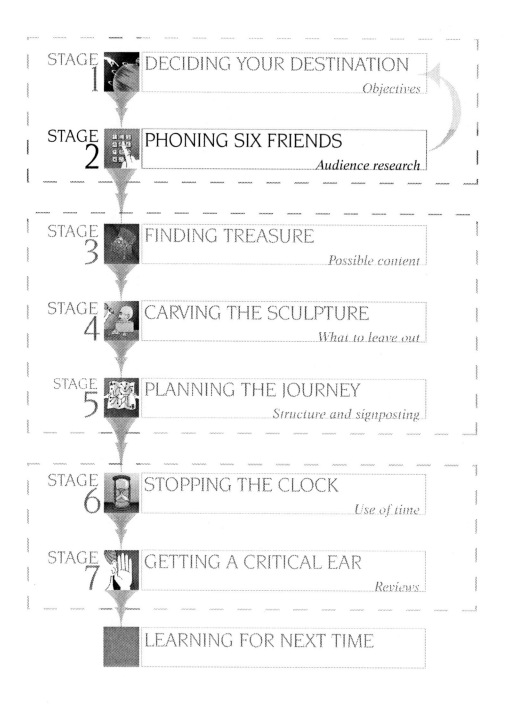

STAGE 1 DECIDING YOUR DESTINATION
Objectives

STAGE 2 PHONING SIX FRIENDS
Audience research

STAGE 3 FINDING TREASURE
Possible content

STAGE 4 CARVING THE SCULPTURE
What to leave out

STAGE 5 PLANNING THE JOURNEY
Structure and signposting

STAGE 6 STOPPING THE CLOCK
Use of time

STAGE 7 GETTING A CRITICAL EAR
Reviews

LEARNING FOR NEXT TIME

– 2 –

PHONING SIX FRIENDS   How to discover as much as you possibly can about the audience so that you can tailor your message as closely as possible to their needs.

Stage 2

So now you have some idea of what you want your audience to **think, feel, say** and **do**, but to make progress you need to know who your audience actually are.

For Single Point Communication, audience research is the most important stage in preparing your message. Stage 1 – *deciding your destination* cannot be properly completed without it. Together, Stages 1 and 2 will create the foundation of your communication.

As with Stage 1, you can spend five minutes, five hours or even five days working on this stage of the process. It is up to you and it will depend to a large extent on the importance of the piece of communication. If it is important enough you will make the time, if it isn't you will not.

Applying Stage 2 rigorously will mean you:

- Discover more about the audience
- Understand the context in which they will receive your message
- Are forewarned of potential issues that could affect your communication

Why 'phoning six friends' really matters

"People buy for their reasons, not yours"
(Ray Orvill Wilson)

The more you know about the audience, the more you can focus on them. Use your time to address *their* issues, rather than risk boring them with information that neither interests them nor matters to them.

Because this is Single Point Communication where you are preparing to interact with a specific audience at a particular point in time, you need to know where that audience is at the start of your interaction. You must know *their* starting point in order give them the right information to move them to the place that you need them to be at the end of your interaction.

If you have already put the principles in Stage 1 into practice, then I am sure you will have found how much the **think, feel, say** and **do** questions encourage you to put yourself in the audience's shoes. And the only way to do that is to find out as much about your audience as you possibly can.

Stage 2 is vital because it helps you to:

- Understand what your audience need to **think, feel** and **say**
- Address their needs and show them why they should listen
- Put the information across in a way that works for them

The tool – phoning six friends

Asking for information is easy enough to understand, but it can be surprisingly difficult to do. All you have to do is ask the person who has involved you to tell you more about the people who will be in the audience you are addressing, the people you are meeting or the person to whom you are writing.

In my experience, if you set yourself a target of speaking to just six people you will get a wealth of useful information, even if three of the people cannot help you at all!

To make your research more productive follow these simple steps, if possible do it working with one or two colleagues:

1 – Brainstorm what you know already

- Write down everything that you already know about the audience, even if the information does not seem relevant to your communication right now.
- Include everything you know about their likes and dislikes, hobbies and interests, past roles and experience.
- If you are faced with larger audiences such as at conferences and seminars, you could put down your assumptions based on the stereotypes you expect to encounter as well as your past experience. For example the delegates at a conference for accountants are likely to be keen on details and numbers, but will the same work with a conference for sales people? Probably not. Similarly if you are addressing a group of senior business people and you are using an analogy relating to cars you would probably talk about luxury cars, rather than cheaper, small cars.

2 – Brainstorm what you would like to find out

Think of yourself as beginning with a blank canvas. You are going to fill it with as much information as it would be useful to know.

- Capture everything you can think of, even if your immediate response is that you could not possibly find out the answer.
- Stretch yourself, set a target of noting down at least 20 –30 things that you would like to find out or know more about.
- When you have completed the brainstorm you may find that one of your colleagues already knows the answer to some of the questions. If they do you can add more to your 'what you know already' brainstorm.

- Group the remaining questions into related areas, it does not matter what groups you choose. You just need to focus on something they have in common. It will make your research easier.

If you want another prompt for questions, I have prepared a list of 30 possible questions you could ask in Appendix 3. A copy can be downloaded from http://www.beclear.co.uk/hints.htm.

3 – Brainstorm who could possibly give you the answers

Whilst there is a wealth of published information that can help with your research, my focus is on getting you to actually talk to people who know the things that won't be in the public domain.

- Examples of people who could be your 'friend' for this particular presentation, document or meeting are:
    - The conference organiser
    - The person who issued the Invitation to Tender
    - The client's Personal Assistant
    - Your boss
    - Your peers
    - A colleague who works in a similar way to your audience
    - The person who provided the introduction or got you the meeting
    - Also, as a businessperson you probably know at least 400 other people in your personal network; one of them might know the answer to your questions, or may know someone else who does.

4 – Match what you need to know with who could give you the answers

Combining the results of Steps 2 & 3 will give you a pretty good starting point for your quest for more information about your audience. Have a look at what you want to find out and then see which 'friend' is most likely to be able to answer that question.

5 – *Pick up the telephone, or walk down the corridor to a colleague*

Once you know which questions you are going to ask which friends start talking to them and make comprehensive notes of everything they tell you. They may say something that seems really insignificant at the time, but by the time you have spoken to some of your other 'friends' it suddenly might be rather more important.

Design Principles Template – audience research

As in Stage 1, you might like to complete the information that you have and that you would like to find out in the second part of the Design Principles Template. A blank copy is shown on the next page and a copy can be downloaded from http://www.beclear.co.uk/hints.htm.

Remember that this part of the Design Principles Template will keep changing for two reasons:

- As you talk to your 'friends' you will find the answers to some of your questions, so the answers will move into the 'what we know already' box.
- The more you find out, the more you may want to find out even more, so there will be new questions to go into your 'what we would like to know' box.

Design Principles Template – audience research

Presentation to / meeting with _____ **in** _____, _____

What we know already about the audience:

-
-
-
-
-
-
-
-

What we would like to know:

-
-
-
-
-
-
-

Who could possibly give us the answers:

-
-
-
-
-
-
-
-

Examples

Talk to your sponsor

"The guy who got us the meeting is our mate."

The above phrase is what two clients, Richard and Andy, said when I asked how they had got the chance to present to a team meeting in a major consultancy.

The presentation really mattered to Richard and Andy because there were only about 12 potential buyers for their product in the country – this consultancy was one of them.

My next question was to ask what their mate, Steve, had told them about the team to which they would be presenting. It transpired that Steve had not told them anything, but then Richard and Andy admitted they had not thought to ask. However, they were going out for a drink with Steve that evening, so I left them armed with a list of questions to ask Steve about his colleagues.

The next morning I went back to my clients, eagerly expecting a wealth of useful information to be waiting for me. You can imagine my reaction when they said: "We didn't get round to your questions – the footie came on." Thankfully there was a 'but' and Richard added "Steve says you can call him direct and ask anything that will help – he really wants us to look good in front of his team."

This is the reality. When someone sticks their neck out and introduces you they want you to succeed. By implication your failure would also be their failure. So if you politely ask that person for some time with them to get background information they will usually be delighted to help. In this particular case, I got a superb profile of everyone in the audience, their educational background, their specialisms and experience in the consultancy; their main challenges and concerns at that time, as well as lots of other useful snippets.

The result was that Richard and Andy were able to really tailor their message to the needs of the six people that they were addressing on that day. Those six people had the potential to be the first step to their first sale.

Key point

Your sponsor will want you to succeed, ask for their help and you will often be surprised at how helpful they are. Prepare your questions before speaking to them, as you may only have one opportunity.

Start a dialogue

"But it says we can't ask questions."

This is what Debbie told me when I asked if she had tried to get any more information from the company who had issued her with the tender document.

Whilst Debbie was correct in terms of what was said in the Invitation to Tender, reality is often very different.

Some companies will answer questions, but they may also reserve the right to publish your questions together with the answers they give in response to all the other bidders as this ensures fairness. In many cases though background information can be gleaned all the same. Sometimes you can also find out much, much more.

In Debbie's case there were inconsistencies in the document that she needed to have clarified in order to prepare a good response. So, Debbie had a valid reason for contacting the company. But before she did we also considered what else it would be useful to know and whether she should try and get all this information at once.

The Invitation to Tender was issued about six weeks before the final submission date, so over a period of about four weeks Debbie spoke to the person who had issued the tender several times on the phone and by email. Although she had never met the person, or worked with the company before, by the time we were finalising the response Debbie had developed such rapport with her contact that she had even been told what the company was expecting to pay!

Key point

Start a dialogue and develop the relationship. You never know where it might lead.

Ask anyone!

"I can't 'phone six friends' because I don't know who the audience is."

Sam approached me saying the above phrase after one of my talks.

He was in a dilemma as his company was applying for an award. They had been short-listed and he had to make the final presentation to the judges, but the names of the judges were secret. Understandably Sam was struggling to see how he could apply my *'phoning six friends'* tool.

My suggestion was to *phone six friends* anyway. I told Sam that if he did not know who to phone, he was to phone anyone who would be pleased to hear from him. I suggested that he explain his dilemma and see what they suggest.

I also prompted Sam a little more, as Marketing Director of a FTSE 100 company he knew lots of people. I asked the following questions and they turned out to be key:

> "Who could you speak to at your previous company who might possibly know?"

> "Who do you know at the major business schools?"

> "Who do you know who writes on this subject?"

> "Who were last years judges? So who would you use in their place?"

Within a few minutes, Sam had thought of three or four people who could probably help him. He phoned me the next afternoon to say he already knew who three of the judges would be and had plenty more 'friends' to phone to get even more background information about them as well as the identities of the remaining judges.

Key point

If you don't know who to talk to try six people at random.

Questions, questions

Because people are so very unique and hence audiences are so very different, I think it is impossible to come up with a definitive list of questions that you might want answering. However, the list of 30 possible question in Appendix 3 is a starting point. A copy can be downloaded from http://www.beclear.co.uk/hints.htm.

Some of the main areas to consider are shown below, together with an explanation of the sort of insights that you can gain from the answers.

What is important to them?

What matters / is important to them is the most fundamental question when preparing for a meeting or presentation. Keep asking this question and follow up with questions such as:

- And what else is important to them?
- What are their hot buttons / green buttons?

Related questions could be

- What are their emotional drivers?
- What will help them politically within their organisation?

Most decisions are made for far more emotional or political reasons than we care to admit. Look at advertising and think about the work of most marketing departments, it is usually designed to appeal to our emotions and aspirations, rather than logic.

The political aspect is more about what the person can gain in terms of their position in the organisation "How can we help them to use this to their advantage?" Alternatively it may help to look at the pressures they face "How could we use this to get the boss / board / media off their back?"

If you can find the answers to these questions you can hone down your message to exactly what the audience needs to hear.

What type of person are they?

There are many, many different ways of considering personality types. Popular indicators include Myers Briggs, Merrill Reid and Insights. Considering your audience in terms of its overall personality can be very helpful. But watch out! It can also be dangerous. You see everyone is unique and may not fit the stereotype you pick as much as you expect.

So with that warning in mind, some things it could be useful to know include:

- "Does the audience like lots of detail, or are they more of a 'big picture' person?"
- "Are they more likely to move towards an opportunity or more likely to move away from a threat?"

The more you know about the personalities of the audience and how they like to receive information the more you can ask people who operate in a similar way how you should put your message across. For example, I naturally have a very structured, detail orientated approach; if I am meeting someone whom my research tells me hates detail, I will ask one of my 'detail hating' colleagues to help with my preparation.

What are their expectations?

You need to know the answer to questions like:

- What do they know about us / our boss / our organisation?
- What are they expecting?
- What are their preconceptions / misconceptions?
- What have they heard about the topic?
- How have I / we been positioned?

Even if you have not met the person before they will have formed some pre-conceptions about you. I remember my first meeting with a prospective client who had been contacted by our telemarketing company. At the end of the meeting we were hired for a small piece of work. The client said they would give us a try because in their words: "you sent us a very professional cold-call letter, which was followed up by a very professional telemarketing call and you've been as professional as we expected today." So, even before I arrived, the potential client had expectations based on letters and phone calls from weeks or maybe months before.

What power or influence do they have?

If your audience does not have the power to buy or say yes to your proposition then you need to know this at the start of your meeting or presentation, not at the end. The message to an influencer will usually be very different from the message to a buyer.

Even if you are told the person has the power to buy, check and double check not only that they have the power, but also that they are prepared to use that power.

What frame of mind will they be in?

A meeting with the Sales Director just after the notorious weekly grilling by the Chief Executive is likely to find them in a very different frame of mind to a meeting just after they have hosted a celebratory lunch for the top performing sales team.

Whilst diaries and circumstances can change, forewarned is forearmed and building a good relationship with your audience's Personal Assistant will always pay dividends.

Who else will be at the meeting?

This is such a simple, obvious little question, but the answer can have significant consequences.

Some years ago I worked with Helen, a senior executive preparing a presentation for her Chief Executive. Work was well under way six weeks before the event and Helen's audience research was ongoing. About a week before the presentation my client discovered that the Finance Director would also be at the meeting. Helen had not been told this before simply because it was accepted practice for presentations like this one. Everyone she spoke to assumed Helen knew that a full briefing with the Chief Executive meant that the Finance Director would be sitting in. Everyone knew except Helen.

This might still appear fairly innocuous until you know that the presentation had four elements to it and as the Chief Executive was interested in the really strategic stuff Helen had put that first. The problem was that the first topic was also financially weak (and that is being generous). The Finance Director would have dug into the financial detail of the first topic so much that Helen would probably never have got as far as the second topic.

Once Helen knew who was attending we worked to completely re-cut the presentation to meet the needs of both members of the audience and make sure that Helen achieved her objectives.

How likely are they to go off at a tangent?

This is particularly pertinent for one-to-one meetings. If you know the audience is likely to dart about and go off at tangents you can prepare appropriately.

You can also prepare yourself so that you give the audience the flexibility they need, whilst being comfortable that you are still in control and can bring them back to the agenda where necessary. (See Chapter 6 – *stopping the clock*, for more about how to do this).

For a conference or seminar what else do I need to know?

Talking to the conference organiser and getting them on your side by working to their deadlines is a really good start. Some of the other more specific things to find out include:

- Who else is speaking and what will they say?
- Is anyone talking about related topics or the same topic?
- When will I be speaking?

The answers to all of these will help you hone your message. It is also useful to check what the audience will be expecting, so ask:

- What billing have I been given?
- What does the programme say I am talking about?
- What does my biography say about me?

I have known more than one client who has wandered quite a lot from the original brief in the six months between agreeing to speak and getting down to preparing the speech a couple of weeks before!

Also, check about the technical side of the event and if there is the opportunity to rehearse at the venue take it. You do not want to be remembered as the speaker who obviously did not know which lectern they should use.

Making 'phoning six friends' work for you

Phoning six friends is an easy tool for those people who are at their best chatting to people; gossiping, exchanging news and gathering information. Others amongst us, myself included, find this simple task more daunting. I know I suffer from what is sometimes called '10 ton telephone syndrome'! I just cannot seem to lift up that receiver, I keep procrastinating and finding more urgent things to do. Whichever type of person you are, it is worth bearing in mind the following:

- **Allow yourself enough time** – some of your key friends and contacts will be out or on holiday or too busy to spare the time at the moment that you call. So try not to leave *phoning six friends* until the last minute.

- **Think through what you want to know** – if you have to contact someone more than a couple of times you risk annoying or even alienating them.

- **Do not overlook those closest to you** – there is often a wealth of information in your own team's, or your boss's heads. If you say you do not want to let them down, even the busiest person will usually find time for you.

- **Co-ordinate your approach with other contributors** – if other people may be contacting the same people with the same questions, work with them to save everyone's time and effort.

- **Thank your 'friends' and offer help in return** – with people you know well the promise of 'a pie and a pint' or a 'coffee and a Danish pastry' next time you meet will often be all you need to do to say thank you, but it is worth asking if there is any way that you can help the other person in return.

Remember, even if you have not spoken to someone for years he or she will probably be flattered that you have called, not only because you have remembered them, but also because you value their opinion enough to have made the call. Spend a few minutes chatting and catching up before gently saying something like:

"I know this is a bit cheeky but I am *presenting to / bidding for / meeting with* . . . And I seem to remember that you used to *work for them / be involved in* . . . so could you possibly spare me a few minutes to talk that through, either now or sometime soon?" And remember, say it with a smile!

A word about tackling the '10 ton telephone'

My strategy is to start by phoning someone I know will be pleased to hear from me, a real 'phone a friend'. Then once I have made the first call it is much easier to move onto other contacts and even people I have never spoken to before whom one of my other 'friends' or contacts have suggested that I call.

No time for 'phoning six friends'

The risk if you do not have time for this Stage is that you prepare a presentation that does not meet the needs of the audience because you did not spend enough time researching them. Strategies for overcoming the time barrier include:

- **Cut the amount of time you were going to spend preparing the presentation or document** – spend it on research instead. Most people spend too little time on audience research and setting objectives, then they have to spend longer than they should on writing or preparing.

- **Use email instead of the phone** – you can contact people by email rather than by phone, but there is a risk of offending them as they may view it that 'you can't even be bothered to pick up the phone'. You are certainly running a risk if you write one email and send it to six people!
- **Ask the next six people you speak to** – this could be at home or at work. Just tag on the end of your conversation something like "whilst we are talking, do you know anything about. . .".

What next?

Now that you are armed with lots of information about your audience go back to Stage 1 – *deciding your destination*, and use the information that you have gathered to refine your objectives. This will probably lead you to more questions about your audience, which is a good thing because the aim is for you to understand as much as possible about the people you will be speaking to.

When you are comfortable with your audience research and your objectives, go on to Chapter 3 – *finding treasure*, but keep checking your audience research as you go along.

If you have been working alone so far, you should consider one other point at this time. You really should get some independent feedback before you go any further. Even talking through the objectives and audience research with someone who knows nothing about your topic or the audience is bound to help you clarify things in your own mind and will usually bring valuable insights.

CASE STUDIES – STAGE 2

Boffin the Inventor

Boffin continued to work with his friend Igor for Stage 2 of the process. Igor thinks that they probably need to know a lot more, but agrees with Boffin that this will be a good start, particularly as Boffin has time to speak to all his 'friends' at some length.

Boffin initially wanted to speak to the conference organiser and five other inventors including Igor. However, Igor suggested he think a little more widely as if he were inventing a new product. After a little more thought Boffin decided to include Patrick from the PR Company that got him the speaking slot. He also agreed that it might be worth talking to his sister Sally. She works in marketing. Boffin doesn't understand what she is talking about a lot of the time, but he agreed with Igor that she might be worth a quick call!

After they had completed Stage 2 they filled in the Design Principles Template:

Presentation to the Automotive Industry Conference in Japan, May 20xx

What we know already about the audience:

- 500 people from around the world
- All involved in the automotive industry
- May be tired as there is an industry awards dinner the night before

What we would like to know:

- What time of day I am speaking?
- Who is speaking before me?
- Who is speaking after me?
- What are the other speaker topics?
- What facilities are there for audience participation?
- What audio / visual equipment is available?
- Are any of the speakers talking about similar / competing products?
- What do they already know about my product?
- What do they know about me and my other inventions?
- What is their general attitude to things invented outside their industry?
- Will they understand my technical terms?
- Are they just representatives of the major manufacturers, or will suppliers be represented too?
- What functions will be represented? (for example manufacturing, I.T., sales and marketing, purchasing)
- Will they be managers or directors?
- What are the demographics of the audience? (male / female split; average age and so on)
- How open are they to innovative presentations?
- What do they expect or like from speakers based on previous events?
- Will they have the power to enter negotiations themselves or will they have to defer to Head Office?
- What types of personality are dominant in the industry?
- What issues is the automotive industry facing at the moment?
- How will they view the product?
- How can I show that it will benefit them?
- What matters to them about new products? (for example defect rates, cost, quality, delivery times, environmental impact)
- What is their attitude to risk?
- Who can I speak to who has presented to this type of audience before?

Who could possibly give us the answers:

- The conference organiser
- Igor, the friend who suggested that I use this process
- The two inventors who helped with engineering the prototypes
- Patrick at the PR company
- Sally, my sister

PHONING SIX FRIENDS

Peter the Project Manager

Peter worked through Stage 2 of the process with Chris. They came up with quite a long list of questions, which in itself helped Peter to start thinking differently about what he actually needs to communicate in the meeting.

He also realised that he had several 'friends' that he could approach including his colleagues Dolores and Tim. Peter gets on well with both of them and had already noticed that they seem to have much more effective communication with Sarah than he has. Other potential sources of information are Pippa, an old colleague who worked with Sarah when Sarah first joined the company, and Jerry, a mate of Peter's who runs a similar sized department at the local council.

At the end Peter completed the Design Principles Template for audience research:

Update meeting with Sarah, April 20xx

What we know already about Sarah:

- She is really bright and has been promoted quickly through the company
- She is very well thought of
- She is direct and to the point
- She manages a really large department very efficiently

What we would like to know:

- What personality type is she?
- What style of presentation / meeting does she prefer?
- Does she 'go off at tangents' and not hear important information when other people have meetings with her?
- Does she like information in tables, graphs or pictures?
- Does she like formal presentations or two-way dialogue?
- What type of pre-meeting information or brief does she like?
- When is a good time to send pre-meeting information?
- What type of post-meeting summary does she like?
- Who is she seeing before me?
- What is she doing after my meeting with her?
- How likely is it that our meeting will be shortened?
- What are her short-term goals?
- What are the main challenges that she is facing at the moment?

- What matters to her?
- How is her performance measured?
- What are her targets?
- What are her 'hot buttons'?
- How can I help Sarah to achieve more?
- How important is my work to her?
- What other information does she get from other sources about my project?
- How important is my major project in terms of other things that are happening in the company?
- How high is the risk of failure of this project to the department?
- How high is the risk of failure of this project to Sarah's position in the company?
- What is her opinion of me?
- What does she want from me?
- How do I fit into her view of the department?
- What are her interests outside work?
- What is she passionate about?
- What makes her laugh?

Who could possibly give us the answers:

- Sarah's Personal Assistant
- Chris, my partner
- Dolores and Tim from my department
- Pippa, my old colleague who used to work with Sarah
- Jerry who runs a large department at the local council

Chrystal and Christof the Creativity Consultants

Whilst time was obviously short with the final meeting less than three working days away, Chrystal and Christof worked through Stage 2, again with Mike facilitating. They actually had a lot of knowledge from their months of discussion. Because of their short timescales Mike encouraged them to do Stage 2 fairly quickly but to keep noting things as they remembered other information that they had received over the months but had never bothered to write down.

Mike helped them to see that whilst they did know a lot, there was also far more that they could and should find out before the presentation. Two other members of the business, Tricia and Trevor, had also worked on the proposition so they soon called on them to see what else they knew. Also they decided that Christof should try and call his old college friend Tanya who had worked in central government ever since leaving university. There were also all the members of the Board that will award the contract, they have quite a good relationship with four of them.

In well under an hour they had the following answers to the questions in Stage 2:

Final presentation to the Board responsible for the Creativity Programme, March 20xx

What we know already about the Board:

- It is made up of five people
- All of them are of managerial level
- Three are male, two are female
- All are aged between 45 – 60 years old
- They have all been in government departments most of their working life
- We have spoken to four of the five people – the one we do not know will Chair the Board
- Christof used to work with one of the Board before he founded the Creativity Consultants
- We are presenting last

- All of them have shown a very exact and methodical approach to the process
- All the Board have very limited knowledge of 'creativity' as a tool to improve the workplace except for the person who used to work with Christof
- All the potential suppliers are presenting on the same day
- They view us as the least experienced as our company hasn't been going as long as the others
- They have to make a decision very soon or they will lose the funding that they have available

What we would like to know:

- Who are the real influencers within the Board?
- What is the person we haven't met like?
- How much say do the respective members of the Board have?
- What do the various panel members like about our proposal?
- What do they like about the other proposals?
- What are their concerns about embarking on this project?
- What would they like us to focus on in this presentation?

- What really matters to them?
- What style of presentation do the members of the Board prefer?
- How do we stand out from our competitors?
- Would the Board prefer to hear more from Chrystal or from Christof?
- How comfortable are the Board with the whole concept of 'creativity'?
- What size is the meeting room?
- What will be the layout of the room?
- Do they really understand our terms and the concepts that we have put forward?

Who could possibly give us the answers:

- The person who issued the Invitation to Tender and is controlling the whole supplier selection process
- Kevin, the member of the Board who once worked with Christof
- Mike
- Other members of the team at the Creativity Consultants, particularly Tricia and Trevor
- Tanya, one of Christof's old college friends who works in central government

BE CLEAR SEVEN STAGE PROCESS™

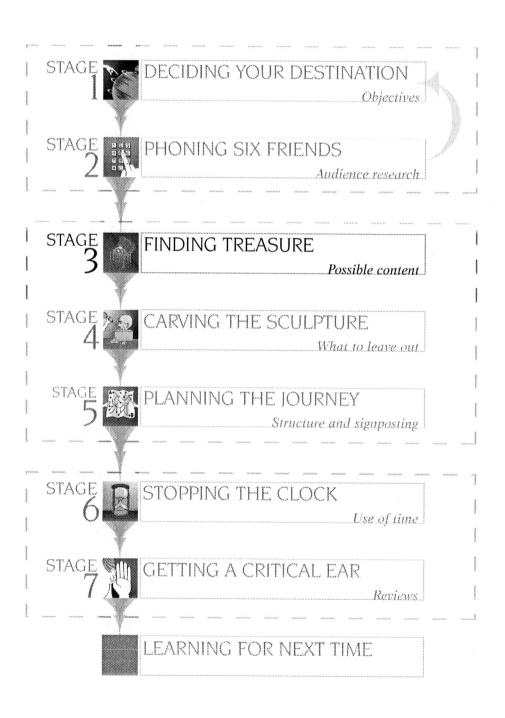

STAGE 1 — DECIDING YOUR DESTINATION
Objectives

STAGE 2 — PHONING SIX FRIENDS
Audience research

STAGE 3 — FINDING TREASURE
Possible content

STAGE 4 — CARVING THE SCULPTURE
What to leave out

STAGE 5 — PLANNING THE JOURNEY
Structure and signposting

STAGE 6 — STOPPING THE CLOCK
Use of time

STAGE 7 — GETTING A CRITICAL EAR
Reviews

LEARNING FOR NEXT TIME

– 3 –

FINDING TREASURE How to gather all the
content you could possibly include in your presentation or
meeting, without evaluating it!

Stage 3

When you have completed Stages 1 and 2 you will know about your audience; who they are and how they would like you to communicate with them. You should also know what you need them to **think** and **feel** and **say**, in order to do what you want them to **do**.

Now you need to work out what content to include in order to help them to that destination. The question Stage 3 starts to answer is:

'What do you need to say in your presentation in order to achieve your objectives?'

This chapter considers Stage 3 of the process. It shows you how to find and gather 'treasure'. In this context 'treasure' means all the content you could *possibly* include. Do not evaluate the content at all in this stage, just think as widely as possible and capture every single idea that comes to you – even if some of them appear to be outside your scope. Chapter 4 will show you how to evaluate your 'treasure' in order to decide what to include and most importantly what to leave out.

Just before you read on to discover the tools that can help you to gather up lots of great information to include in your presentation, I need to give you a word of warning about what this stage is *not*!

What this chapter is not about

Do not kid yourself that you can get away with taking two or three existing presentations and cobbling them together. The audience can and usually do see the join. Also, doing this will not achieve the objectives that you have set out in your Design Principles. How can they when the old presentations were designed for a different audience at a different time with different needs?

So bear with me and give what I talk about in this chapter a try. You really will find it quicker and easier in the long run and your audience will thank you for it.

The more widely and creatively you think in Stage 3:

- The fewer rewrites and amendments you will need
- The more powerful your stories and analogies will be
- The more likely you are to include all the information the audience needs to hear

Why 'finding treasure' really matters

"The best way to have a good idea is to have lots of ideas." (Linus Pauling)

'Finding treasure' is important because without it you are unlikely to have all the information the audience needs. Yet even when you are aware of this fact it is unlikely that you will realise anything is missing. This is because it is difficult to consider a subject that you know well from the point of view of your audience. It is hard to read the minds of an unfamiliar audience, and is perfectly normal.

Stage 3 is vital because:

- You need to think as widely as possible about your topic to find all the information that could be useful for your audience
- As an expert you tend not to realise how much you take for granted
- The audience often *needs* to know stuff that you *think* they already know

The tools – finding treasure

There are many tools and techniques that overlap and interlink in the two broad areas of:

- Where to find treasure
- How to store treasure once you have found it

The secret is to be aware of the different tools you have available to find this 'treasure'. Then with a flexible approach you can use the tools that are most appropriate to your current situation. If you are thinking that it all sounds like a bit of a treasure hunt – it is!

There are three tools that I find particularly useful. I call them:

- Big space for big ideas
- Questions, questions, questions
- Read it to find it

I will begin by sharing with you the tool that I find the most exciting and productive when working with my clients. This is what I recommend you do when you have some quality thinking time available to devote to finding the content that your audience needs to know.

I will then go on to describe the other two tools that you need to be aware of. In this way, with three tools to choose from you will have a complete range to use according to the situation.

Tool 1 – Big space for big ideas

This is a way of 'finding treasure' from the source that most people use; their own heads. But it differs significantly from the usual method people use to come up with ideas for a presentation – they sit at a computer screen and type a list of all the information and ideas they can think of.

You really can find valuable treasure without leaving the office. You will find it in that most fertile of places . . . your mind!

Start by giving yourself some space to do this; space in terms of time, space in terms of your head and space in terms of the room. Ideally you need a large blank wall or a huge table. If you can ask a colleague to join you and do this together, then do. Two heads are invariably better than one.

1 – Get ready

- Put a piece of brown paper about 750mm (2.5 ft) deep and 3 meters (10 ft) long onto a wall (floor or table) where you can not only see the whole sheet at once, but that you can get to every section of it easily. You can get rolls of brown paper that are this size from any good stationers.

- Get a supply of moveable notes such as Post-it® notes. I usually use the standard size of 76mm x 127mm, but any size will do, you can even use the fun ones shaped like flowers or speech bubbles – whatever you prefer. Just make sure they are large enough to write on so that you can read it when standing back and looking at everything on your brown paper.

- Get some different coloured felt-tip pens to write with.

2 – Brainstorm all the possible content you could include

- The aim is to capture all the information that you think should be included and a lot more besides.
- Remember this is a brainstorm so you may have ideas that are repeated or overlap, as well as some that are very high level and others that are very detailed.
- Write each idea that you have, as it comes to you on a separate Post-it® note and stick it anywhere on the left hand side of your brown paper at random.
- Later you will move the ideas around, so it is important to have each one on a separate note.

3 – Take a break

- Go for a walk or a get a cup of coffee.
- The aim is to return with a fresh perspective.

*4 – Brainstorm all the information your audience might possibly be interested in **knowing***

- To do this you need to 'put yourself in the audience's shoes', so look at the output from Stage 2 – *phoning six friends.* It will be on your Design Principles Template.
- Again use Post-it® notes to record each of your ideas, but this time put them on the right hand side of your brown paper.
- Keep reminding yourself of what you know about the audience from *phoning six friends.*

5 – Compare the results of Step 2 and Step 4

- Match the ideas that you have written on your notes. Any topics that are included in both brainstorms need putting together. All the areas that were included in both Steps 2 and 4, will almost certainly need including.
- Any topics that you found in Step 4 *alone* may need including.
- Any topics that you found in Step 2 *alone* may not need including.

We will look at how to decide what to include and what to leave out in Chapter 4.

Advantages of the 'Big space for big ideas' tool

- You (and your colleagues) can see all the possible content at a glance.
- It is easy to keep everything you have discussed in your conscious mind as it is all visible at once.
- It is a simple tool that most people can understand quickly and easily.
- Your energy levels will be higher if you put the brown paper on the wall and stand up at it and move around, rather than hunch or crouch over a table or floor. By moving you will tend to be more creative.
- The format is ideal for Stages 4 and 5 of the process.

Disadvantages of the 'Big space for big ideas' tool

- Finding available wall space may be a challenge if you work in an open plan office, or if like me you often work whilst travelling on trains and planes. There are solutions – in the office try using a flip chart if one is available, whilst for trains and planes use mini Post-it® notes and stick them on pieces of A4 or A3 copy paper.

Tool 2 – Questions, questions, questions

This is similar to the 'Big space for big ideas' tool. You still work with a colleague in a big space with brown paper and moveable notes. The difference is in the questions that you use. This time you ask yourself 'what questions could the audience possibly want answering?'

1 – Brainstorm the possible questions

- Your aim is to think of all the possible questions your audience could have about your subject.
- Write each question on a different movable note.
- Place each note on the brown paper at random.

2 –   Brainstorm the answers to the questions

- Again use Post-it® notes, but ideally of a different colour so that they are easy to differentiate from those used earlier.
- Place the appropriate answer(s) alongside the relevant questions.

3 –   Brainstorm any more questions that the audience might have as a result of the answers generated in Step 2

- Look at each answer and ask yourselves whether the answer would cause the audience to have more questions. Would the audience want to delve deeper given their concerns or priorities or will they be happy with the level of detail you are giving them? Only you can decide.
- Write each of these additional questions on separate Post-it® notes.

4 –   Repeat the process

- Generate the answers to the second set of questions as you did for Step 2, above.
- Place the appropriate answer(s) alongside the relevant questions.
- Repeat this question and answer process until you have exhausted the subject and run out of questions.

When to use the 'Questions, questions, questions' tool

- The advantages and disadvantages are the same as for 'Tool 1 – Big space for big ideas'.
- The difference between the two tools, however, is in the prompts for your brainstorm or idea generation.
- There is no set rule about when to use one or the other. It is simply decided by the subject matter and / or your personal preference.

Tool 3 – Read it to find it

Sometimes the only option open to you will be to read documents to find the material you need. For example, when someone wants you to write a presentation for them and they don't have time to talk to you about the content. Assuming that they give you a comprehensive document or documents about the subject and spend time with you agreeing the Design Principles, including telling you about the audience, then you can get the rest of the information from the document as follows:

1 – Read the document quickly

- In the first instance, skim through the document as this will give you an overview of the content and a feel for what is important.

2 – Highlight key comments, phrases and headings

- Re-read the document, this time much more slowly and carefully.
- Highlight all the areas that you might possibly need to include in your presentation.

3 – Transcribe the highlighted parts onto Post-it® notes

- Write each part you have highlighted in the document available onto separate Post-it® notes.

Stick each Post-it® note onto brown paper or flip charts, or use mini Post-it® notes and put them onto any available A4 or A3 blank paper.

4 – Read more widely

- If you are preparing a presentation on a subject that you do not know (as I often do), be prepared to read far more widely than you might expect.
- For example, I have read magazines about specialist

lending when preparing presentations for a non-standard mortgage provider and motorcycle magazines when working with a company involved in motorcycle design.

- Tear out or photocopy useful articles, highlight key points and add them to your store of possible content.

When to use the 'Read it to find it' tool

If you do not know the subject this process is ideal as long as suitable documents or background material are available.

If the audience have already received a document e.g. a proposal or response to an Invitation to Tender it helps you to overcome the temptation to repeat the document in a verbal format, rather than using only the information that the audience needs to hear and putting it in an order that is best for them.

More ways to store 'treasure'

Storing treasure is about making a note of your ideas as they come to you.

There are lots of ways to do this. If you don't capture an idea immediately there is a danger that you say to yourself: "I must remember that for when I start to prepare the presentation or plan the meeting". Then you find this same idea keeps coming back to you, which is fine, but when you want to remember it, you can't. Also, by now, by suppressing your ideas, you will have inadvertently stopped your subconscious mind coming up with other ideas.

Here are some ways of capturing ideas, particularly the *ad hoc* ideas that come to you when you are lying in the bath, cooking the dinner or walking the dog. They include:

- Using Post-it® notes
- Keeping an ideas book
- Drawing mind maps
- Free / speed writing
- Writing lists

These are explained briefly below:

Using Post-it® notes

Carry a pad of Post-it® notes around with you at all times, even keep one by your bed! Jot each idea that you get onto a separate note.

Advantages of using Post-it® notes

- It is easy and cheap to do.
- The content is in an ideal format for Stage 4 in the process.
- You can keep capturing ideas wherever you are.

Disadvantages of using Post-it® notes

- There aren't any really!

Keeping an ideas book

An ideas book is a notebook that you always carry around with you. Jot any ideas down and use this as a source of ideas and inspiration when you have time set aside for designing your presentation, or planning your meeting.

Advantages of keeping an ideas book

- As with Post-it® notes you can keep capturing content and ideas whenever they occur to you.
- You have all your ideas in one place.

Disadvantages of keeping an ideas book

- Unless you write each idea on a separate page and then rip the pages out of the book you will need to transcribe the ideas into another format before you get to Stage 4 in the process.

I keep both Post-it® notes and an ideas book with me at all times. That way I can put the idea on the Post-it® note first and then stick it in the ideas book so that I have all my ideas together in one place. When I get to the slot in my diary for working on that particular piece of communication I simply transfer the Post-it® notes onto my piece of brown paper.

Drawing mind maps

Mind maps encourage you to think creatively and to include information that may initially appear unrelated to much of the other information. Mind maps use key words, colour and images; they can be drawn by hand or by using mind-mapping software.

For more information about mind mapping see The Mind Map Book by Tony Buzan.

Advantages of drawing mind maps

- They help you to think more creatively than writing a list.

Disadvantages of drawing mind maps

- It can take time and practice to master the art of drawing mind maps if you haven't used them before.
- Some of the information you create in a mind map will need transcribing for the next stage of the process.

Free / speed writing

This is particularly useful when you have lots of information in your head, but cannot begin to sort it into a logical order. Take a blank sheet of paper and simply begin to write whatever is in your head, do not stop to review it or correct it, just force yourself to keep writing at speed until you have exhausted your thoughts.

Once you have done this you will find that your mind has become clearer and you will be able to use any of the usual tools or you can go back and highlight key points as if you were using 'Tool 3 – Read it to find it'.

Advantages of free / speed writing

- It can help you to start generating and capturing ideas if you have so much in your mind that you are feeling overwhelmed and don't know where to begin.

Disadvantages of free / speed writing

- Some duplication of ideas may occur as once you have written everything down you then need to read it through and capture all the ideas on Post-it® notes or in a mind map.

Writing lists

I am sure that you can write or even type a list of topics to include. Many people think it is the only way to capture content! Hopefully by now you can see there are many others.

Advantages of writing lists

- Very few!

Disadvantages of writing lists

- Your list will tend to be in an order that is logical to *you*, rather than the order that is best for the *audience*.

- Once you have a list that is in one logical sequence you will naturally be quite reluctant to spend time finding another logical sequence for it.
- Stages 4 and 5 become much harder, because you have almost jumped to an answer without them.

More types of 'treasure'

When you are 'finding treasure' remember that you are looking for what your audience needs to know in order to do what you want them to **do**. So think more widely than the topic areas and subjects that you consider need to be included. Think of all the different ways that you can put information across including:

- Case studies, stories and analogies
- Facts, figures and statistics
- Pictures, diagrams and graphs
- Props, visual aids and memory prompts

Each of these is explained in more detail below.

Case studies, stories and analogies

Everyone loves stories. Children listen intently to stories. We want to know what happens, who did what and what happened in the end. If you look back across history you will see that stories have always played a great part in imparting knowledge. Think for a moment about parables, as well as great myths, legends and fairytales. There are stories that teach you something, stories with morals and perhaps, most importantly, stories of personal experience.

Using stories will help to bring your business presentation to life and to make it more accessible to the audience.

Think how many ways you could get your point across by using stories. For example, throughout this book I use examples to explain concepts, tools and techniques wherever I think that it will help the reader to grasp ideas more easily.

When you use stories or case studies, make them as meaningful and memorable as possible. For example, a friend of mine was once talking about the different tax implications of running a business as a sole trader, a partnership or a limited company. He could have said:

"Imagine someone owns a shop. If they own it as a sole trader the tax implications will be . . .

But after a few years he marries and decides to make the business a partnership with his partner, so the tax implications will then be . . .

Later still their children join the business and they decide to turn it into a limited company, the tax implications will then be . . ."

Now you can probably relate to this reasonably well, but it could be much richer and more memorable by adding a little bit of detail, as shown in the example below:

"In order to explain the different tax implications, let's follow the life story of a young man called Horace.

Now Horace has a fish and chip shop, in the seaside town of Skegness. To begin with Horace ran the business as a sole trader and the tax implications were . . .

As time went by Horace began dating a young lady by the name of Doris. One day Horace and

Doris decided they were right for each other and they married. At that time Horace made the business into a partnership and the tax implications were . . .

Over time along came two children: Horace Junior and Little Doris. When the children left school they decided to join the family business and so Horace and Doris changed it from a partnership to a limited company and the tax implications were . . ."

Now depending on the audience you might change the names of the characters, the type of shop, the location and so on. The important thing is to make it something that you are comfortable with and that will make it memorable for the audience. So your characters might be names people know from popular culture like Mickey and Minnie or Fred and Wilma; the shop could be a Pizzeria or a high class dress shop; the place could be Greenwich Village, New York or Sleepy Hollow. You will decide what is best based on the audience background you gained in Stage 2 – *phoning six friends.*

Facts, figures and statistics

Hard data can enhance your communication, but it can also be an easy way to bore people. So capture the data that you want to use and then think of ways to make it more accessible and meaningful for people. Take a look at the following examples:

Amazing facts – I support Leicestershire Life Education, an anti-drugs charity that teaches young children how special and unique their bodies are. As part of this they use 'amazing facts' like 'If you take all the blood vessels in an adult human being and put them end to end, how far will they reach. Well, the answer is twice round the world.'

London to Dover – *When my friend, the high performance coach Andy Mouncey talks about the time that he ran from London to Dover as part of a triathlon challenge, he doesn't describe the distance as 87 miles, instead he says it is the equivalent of three and a half marathons. Most people cannot begin to comprehend 87 miles in terms of running, but they know enough to consider a marathon a pretty significant distance, so three and a half marathons back to back is . . . Wow!*

Both these examples make the information easier for the audience to understand and grasp.

Your audience will be able to understand more complex concepts if they are presented in an interesting, simple or memorable way.

Pictures, diagrams and graphs

Many people like to receive information in a visual format. You know the saying 'A picture tells a thousand words'. So, in terms of a business presentation your *picture* could be a diagram or a simple graph.

If you have a good visual image that explains your concept or encapsulates your story, then include it as part of your possible content. Add it to your 'treasure' chest.

Investing in good quality graphics is certainly worth considering, particularly if you could re-use images in later presentations. Give a professional designer a clear brief and you should get a really good visual representation of your concept that can be used time and time again.

When you are presenting to the same audience at occasional intervals, such as to your Board of Directors, or to a team meeting, then using the same strong image as part of the presentation will be a good way to remind them of the subject and help them to recall what you have said in the past. In this way it brands the presentation and keeps things consistent.

In this book I use cartoon images for each of the key stages as I know that many readers will find them more memorable than the words alone.

A quick word of warning! Before we go on I'd like to remind you that your aim should be to give the audience something to *look at*, not something to *read*. A PowerPoint slide full of bullet points may aid the presenter, but it *does not* provide a visual image for the audience! 'Death by PowerPoint' is a commonly heard phrase and it refers precisely to the kind of presentation that has slides that are simply memory joggers for the presenter but offer no added value to the audience.

Props, visual aids and memory prompts

By all means do use props and visual aids. But not your PowerPoint slides for this. I mean that you use something tangible that people can *see* or *touch* such as juggling balls, teddy bears, or building blocks. These are just a few of the many excellent props and visual aids that I have seen people use. Others have included jugs of orange juice poured into tumblers to explain financial information; giant padlocks and keys to illustrate internet encryption and different types of fruit to link to the colours of the rainbow. The list of possibilities is endless, it is limited only by your imagination and your level of confidence when presenting.

Other good prompts for the memory are sounds and smells. Whilst generating and replicating smells is quite difficult, the use of sound is quite easy to arrange these days. The technology to play music or a video is available in most venues, particularly now that there are CD players integrated into laptop computers. However, you need time to find the perfect sound or piece of music.

Be aware that you may need to pay royalties and will probably need a DJ license, but these can both be arranged quite easily. You will need to check the current situation in the country where you are presenting. In the UK contact the Mechanical-Copyright Protection Society (www.mcps.co.uk) and in the US contact ASCAP (www.ascap.com).

The advantage of this type of aural aid for your presentation is that it makes it immediately memorable because it is unusual or different. As the aid should help to explain your concept in a simple way then it will be doubly memorable. Finally it may enable you to inject some humour into your presentation that will lift the audience's energy levels and make them more receptive to new information.

One thing to remember when considering something unusual is that it *must* help explain your message. Audiences are very unforgiving of gimmicks that add no value.

Store your treasure as you go along. Start now!

- Your sub-conscious starts giving you ideas from the very first moment that you know about a particular piece of communication
- Storing ideas as soon as they come to you frees your mind to come up with more of them
- If you already have two or three ideas collected before you spend some quality preparation time, it will get you off to a flying start

Making 'finding treasure' work for you

I have found that spending just half an hour gathering up all the ideas I can think of for possible content *without discarding* anything is quick and easy to do as well as highly fruitful. I know for some people there is the temptation to dive into writing the presentation right away to get a quick result. But I have found that if you are one of those people who wants to just start writing slides and 'cutting and pasting', it is well worth holding back and giving this a try first.

In summary, the key things to remember about Stage 3 are:

- **Think as widely and creatively as possible** – you need to have plenty of content to discard.
- **Remember all ideas are good ideas** – it is especially important to remember this when brainstorming ideas with colleagues as one person's daft idea may spark another person's innovative suggestion or brilliant master-stroke.
- **Store everything** – the time for discarding is in Stage 4 – *carving the sculpture*.
- **Write down ideas as soon as they come to you** – this will free your mind to come up with other ideas.

- **Have a few ideas jotted down before you start** – a blank
  piece of paper can be daunting.

No time for 'finding treasure'

The risk is that if you take an old presentation or report and
make it fit the needs of another audience – it won't work!
With each presentation or meeting you will find yourself
addressing different people at a different time and with a
different objective.

In just half an hour (or even less) you could have most of the
information you need noted in such a way that you can use it
to meet the needs of the audience. You will then find yourself
thinking about your content in a new, more objective way and
will be well on the way to having all the information you need
to help your audience to **think, feel, say** and **do** all the things
that you have set as your Design Principles.

If you really are short of time:

- **Spend five minutes and no more jotting down possible subject
  areas** – ideally use mini Post-it® notes
- **Spend another five minutes and no more noting down possible
  case studies, stories and analogies** – also include facts and
  figures as well as diagrams and images that you already have
- **Capture everything on one piece of paper using Post-it® notes**
  – this way it will all be in your conscious mind

What next?

Go on to Chapter 4 – *carving the sculpture*. Chapter 4 will help you to take all the treasure that you have found and decide what to *leave out*. One of the ways that you can tell whether you have spent enough time on 'finding treasure' is when you have plenty of information to leave out in Stage 4!

Be aware that there may still be more 'treasure' out there – you just haven't found it yet. So keep that pad of Post-it® notes and keep adding any new ideas that you get to your brown paper.

If you have time, give yourself a couple of days before you go on to Stage 4 as you will almost certainly think of other things that you could include as soon as you relax and start focusing on something else. When I am working with clients, I always aim to have at least two or three days' break between Stage 3 – *finding treasure* and Stage 4 – *carving the sculpture*.

CASE STUDIES – STAGE 3

Boffin the Inventor

Boffin worked through Stage 3 of the process on his own. At the end he had the following information on his brown paper:

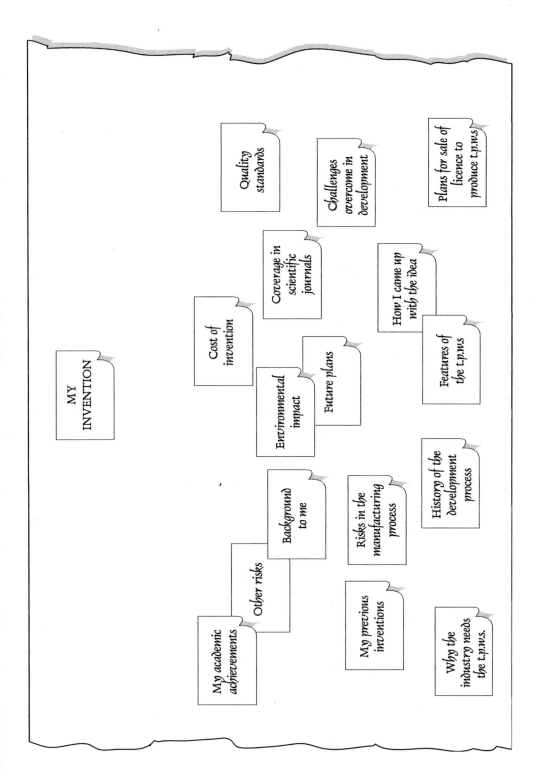

MY INVENTION

Quality standards

Challenges overcome in development

Plans for sale of licence to produce t.p.ws

Coverage in scientific journals

How I came up with the idea

Cost of invention

Features of the t.p.ws

Environmental impact

Future plans

Background to me

Risks in the manufacturing process

History of the development process

Other risks

My academic achievements

My previous inventions

Why the industry needs the t.p.ws.

Peter the Project Manager

Peter continued to work with his partner Chris and together they brainstormed 'finding treasure' to see what could be included in the next update. At the end of Stage 3 they had a brown paper like this:

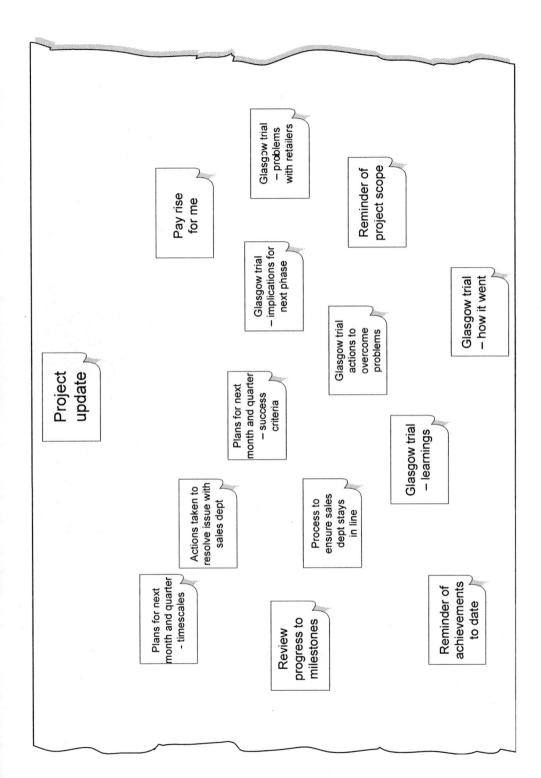

Chrystal and Christof the Creativity Consultants

Mike encouraged Chrystal and Christof to quickly transcribe the broad sections that they were planning to include in their presentation. Despite some resistance he got them to put each section on a different Post-it® note and put it on brown paper as he knew it would be the only way to get them to see the whole picture, rather than their own presentations in isolation. He deliberately mixed up the Post-it® notes so that they didn't have a pre-defined order.

be clear

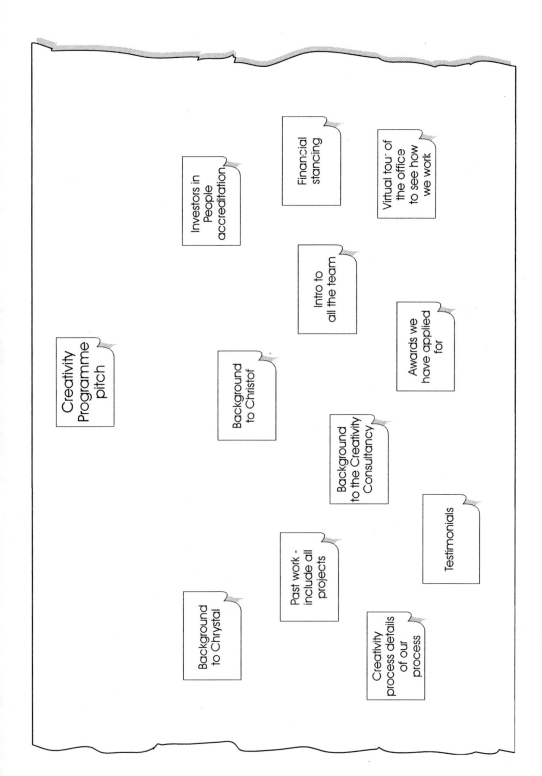

BE CLEAR SEVEN STAGE PROCESS™

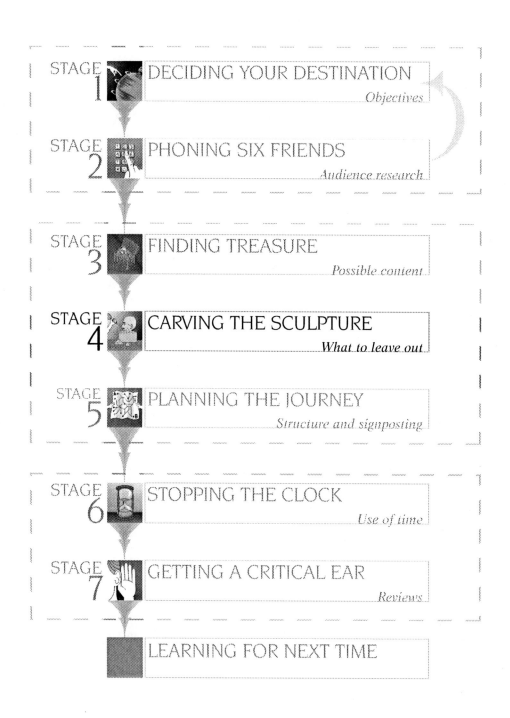

STAGE 1 DECIDING YOUR DESTINATION
Objectives

STAGE 2 PHONING SIX FRIENDS
Audience research

STAGE 3 FINDING TREASURE
Possible content

STAGE 4 CARVING THE SCULPTURE
What to leave out

STAGE 5 PLANNING THE JOURNEY
Structure and signposting

STAGE 6 STOPPING THE CLOCK
Use of time

STAGE 7 GETTING A CRITICAL EAR
Reviews

LEARNING FOR NEXT TIME

– 4 –

CARVING THE SCULPTURE How to use
your Design Principles in order to decide what to include in your
presentation and most importantly, what to leave out.

Stage 4

This stage is all about taking the valuable treasure that you have gathered – that great wealth of possible content – and deciding what the audience does not need to hear *at this particular time*. All information will have a place at some time for one audience or another, but your aim should be to give the audience just enough information to move them to the place that they need to be – nothing more.

Most people find this step difficult because of one small thing – their ego!

We all have an ego. And what ghastly, lily-livered people we would all be without one, but it is important that you leave yours at home on the day when you are deciding what to leave out of your presentation, document or meeting. If not your ego may make you include information that your audience really doesn't need to know.

Think of yourself as a sculptor; perhaps as Michelangelo carving his David, or the ancient Greek who turned a single piece of marble into the Venus de Milo. You have a shapeless piece of marble at the start. It is what you chip away, not what you leave, that will turn it into a beautifully carved statue that will immediately entrance an audience. You must do the same with your presentation. Remember 'less is more'.

Being a ruthless sculptor will mean:

- You only include the information your audience needs to hear
- Your presentation will be more memorable
- Your key points will be clear and concise

Why 'carving the sculpture' really matters

"If I am to speak for ten minutes, I need a week for preparation; if fifteen minutes, three days; if half an hour, two days; if an hour, I am ready now."   (Woodrow Wilson)

Most presentations include too much information; this is also true of documents but to a lesser extent. In some cases it becomes really obvious. For example, if you experience a presentation where the presenter hardly has time to draw breath, where he runs over time or where the audience comes away feeling punch-drunk because they have been swamped with so much information.

Usually the effect is not too noticeable, but the result in terms of the audience's comprehension and understanding is still the same. They simply don't understand parts of the presentation and there is so much *to* remember that the chances are they will forget the important bits.

Most presentations that I listen to have twice as much content as they should for the length of time available. Were speakers to halve the amount of material they have available they would be able to explain, illustrate and reinforce the points they need to make properly and effectively. The audience would then have a far greater chance of understanding, remembering and more importantly *doing* what the speaker needs them to **do**.

When you listen to presentations in future, be aware of how much of the information you really need to hear and how quickly you become bored.

CARVING THE SCULPTURE

Stage 4 is vital because:

- The audience only needs enough information to move them forward to your chosen destination
- The audience isn't the expert, so they may be confused by too much information
- If the information is new to the audience they often need it explaining far more slowly and simply than the speaker expects

The tool – carving the sculpture

This stage is all about only having the information that the audience needs to hear and not a whole lot more. Here each piece of possible content that was found and stored in Stage 3 – *finding treasure* is reviewed against what you want the audience to **think, feel, say** and **do** to see if it should be included or not.

I will explain this tool using brown paper and Post-it® notes as this is my preferred method and I find it works best for most clients. However, it is quite a simple tool so I am sure that you will be able to use mind-maps or lists in a similar way, if you prefer.

This tool is quick and easy to do and it only has three parts, but and this is quite a big *but*, you need to do it rigorously and remember to leave your ego at home!

1 – Focus on your objectives

If you completed the Design Principles Template in Stage 1 – *deciding your destination* then your objectives will be clearly written in the boxes.

Make sure that these are still the things that you need the audience to **think** and **feel** and **say** in order to do what you need them to **do**.

Fix a copy of your Design Principles Template onto one side of your brown paper so that it is easy to see.

2 – Check your content for relevance

Now you are going to consider each piece of possible content to see if it helps you to achieve your objectives. If it *does* you will retain it, if *not* you will put it to one side.

- Take each Post-it® note one at a time and check it against your Design Principles.
- Move the content that *passes* your test towards the centre of your brown paper.
- Content that *fails* the test should be grouped together at the bottom or the side of the brown paper.

Remember that anything you leave out is still important information and you may need to go back to it. Also, you may need to include it elsewhere as we shall see later in the section on 'Overcoming ego and logic'.

3 – Find what you have missed out

- There is often something that has been forgotten.
- Look back at your Design Principles and check that you have content to make your audience **think** all the things you need them to think and **feel** all you need them to feel.
- Add any new content on separate Post-it® notes.
- Adjust your Design Principles if you think that you are not going to aim for that particular objective after all.

Overcoming ego and logic

I have said that it 'helps to leave your ego at home' for this stage. But you may be wondering what I really mean by this and what I mean about overcoming logic.

Ego gets in the way of being a good sculptor if you find yourself saying things like: "but I *like* this", "I'm *attached* to this" or "but this is *important* to me". When logic intervenes you may say things like "but we've always included this bit", "you can't explain it properly without including . . ." or "obviously we need all the figures, not just the headlines".

These phrases usually come out when you are working with someone either collaboratively or with an external reviewer. At times you will believe some of the information is really important but your reviewer may suggest that it shouldn't be included. When that happens think of other, more effective ways that the information can be included, the main ones are:

- Using your sponsor or introducer to put the information across for you.
- Mentioning it and telling the audience to ask if they want to know the detail.
- Including it in the Question and Answer session.

These are explained in the following examples.

Using your introducer

"But, they need to know that I am an expert so that they listen to me. So I have to tell them I was the top performing salesman for five years and hope it doesn't sound conceited."

This was the problem for my client, Tony. Tony was presenting to a group of sales people in a company where he had been a top-performing sales person.

Over the years he had changed roles, and now he needed to present some new initiatives to the sales team. He needed the current sales team to understand that he knew the pressures that they faced and that he had shared their experiences and could empathise with them. He also recognised that there was a strong danger that hearing him say how good he had been could alienate them.

The solution was to get the person who introduced him to explain Tony's background and put it into the right context so that the sales people were receptive to his message. This also meant that Tony saved valuable time in the presentation that he could then devote to his key messages.

Key point

Script what you want your introducer to say about you. That way:

- You can get straight to the heart of your presentation
- Your audience already know why it is important to listen to you
- You can use a third party endorsement rather than start by telling people how good you are

Mentioning it briefly

"My eyes started to glaze over at the part about .
. . in fact I was starting to lose the will to live."

This is a very frank and honest quote from a reviewer and it is usually a sign that there is too much detail in the presentation.

Assuming that you are convinced that the information has to be included, try just mentioning it briefly and telling the audience how they can find out more.

In the following example, my client, Angela, was convinced that she needed to tell her team why they had changed a way of measuring their performance, but the explanation of the underlying ratios was quite complex. Angela asked a colleague and I to help with her preparation for the next team meeting. After discussion we both felt that this level of detail was unnecessary.

Eventually Angela was persuaded to tell the team what the change was and its impact on them, then she said something like "If you would like to know about the actual ratios that are underlying this please ask me at coffee." She expected to be inundated with questions at coffee, but as you have probably guessed, she didn't receive any!

Angela was the expert so her audience trusted her to have made the right decision based on her knowledge and experience. They didn't need or want to go checking up on her.

Key point

If some of the audience *might* want more information but your reviewer thinks it is unlikely try mentioning it briefly and giving the audience the opportunity to ask for more detail. You will be surprised how often no one asks for the detail.

Using the Q&A session

"I know this bit of information doesn't really fit in the presentation, but I can't afford to miss the opportunity to get the message across to such an important audience."

This is what Jez said when he was asked to speak at a business lunch about a particular project with which he was involved. Jez wanted to give the audience some idea of the other work that he was doing, but that information did not really fit with the rest of his presentation.

So, as a first step, Jez gave his introducer a note of how he would like to be introduced, which mentioned that his work involved this project amongst many others. Then, at the end of the talk during the Questions & Answers Jez received a question, which would have benefited from further explanation about his other projects. It was at this point that he said something like: "it might help if I give you a little background to my other work so that you can see how it all fits together." He got several nods of approval from the audience and went on to deliver a few succinct messages about his other work. He had rehearsed this as much as the main presentation.

CARVING THE SCULPTURE

Key point

You can put information into the Q&A session in three ways:

- Plant a question with a friend that you have in the audience
- Introduce the information as part of your answer to another question
- Introduce a question yourself by saying: "something I am often asked about is . . ." or "you might find it helpful if I explain a little more about . . ."

Making 'carving the sculpture' work for you

This is the part that needs constant vigilance. In general the more you take out the better. It is worth persevering and remembering the key things about Stage 4 are:

- **'Less is more'**
- **Leave your ego at home** – you know lots of information about your subject, but the audience only needs to know a little bit.
- **Do not discard anything entirely** – put it on the edge of your brown paper so you can call on it if your objectives change because of your ongoing audience research.

Remember you should have lots of information left over at the end. It could be useful for any of the following situations:

- Questions from your audience
- The next meeting
- Your introduction by the person hosting the meeting or event
- Expert investigations such as due diligence, technical reviews and financial appraisals
- Supporting papers
- Formal proposals

In fact, it could be needed anywhere, but not here. Keep it until you have the right audience at the right time.

No time for 'carving the sculpture'

If you have come this far, you really are committed to finding the time to make your presentation a good one and probably a great one.

This is where spending time on Stages 1 and 2 really pays dividends. If you have researched your audience well and have been thorough in deciding your objectives, then this stage should be quite quick and simple.

When you really are short of time, simply complete Stage 4 a little more quickly than you might like. The main risk here is that you take something out that actually needs leaving in, but that should become obvious in Stage 5 at which point you can always put it back in.

Finding time for 'carving the sculpture' will mean:

- The next stage in the process is quicker and simpler
- Your audience will recognise that you have thought of their needs
- Your presentation will have more impact and less waffle!

What next?

By now, you are well over half way through the process that will enable you to decide what you need to include in your communication to help your audience to **think, feel, say** and ultimately do what you need them to **do**.

Now move on to Chapter 5 – *planning the journey* where you will learn how to put the information into the best order for your audience and how to help your audience to mentally prepare for what you are about to tell them.

CASE STUDIES – STAGE 4

Boffin the Inventor

Boffin asked his friend Igor for some help when he got to Stage 4 of the process. Igor knew that persuading Boffin to leave out a lot of the background would be quite difficult, so he suggested that they also get some help from Boffin's sister Sally. Sally was one of the people Boffin had used when he *phoned six friends* and as Igor was such an old friend of Boffin's he had met Sally several times over the years and felt certain that she would be able to provide a more commercial point of view.

Between them they managed to convince Boffin that the conference audience did not need to know all about the background to the development. They also pointed out that one key thing was missing – the *benefits* of the Turbo Powered Wimbley Stick! Finally they suggested that the conference host would be the best person to highlight Boffin's academic achievements and previous inventions, leaving Boffin to concentrate on selling the concept of the Turbo Powered Wimbley Stick.

At the end of their time together their brown paper looked like this:

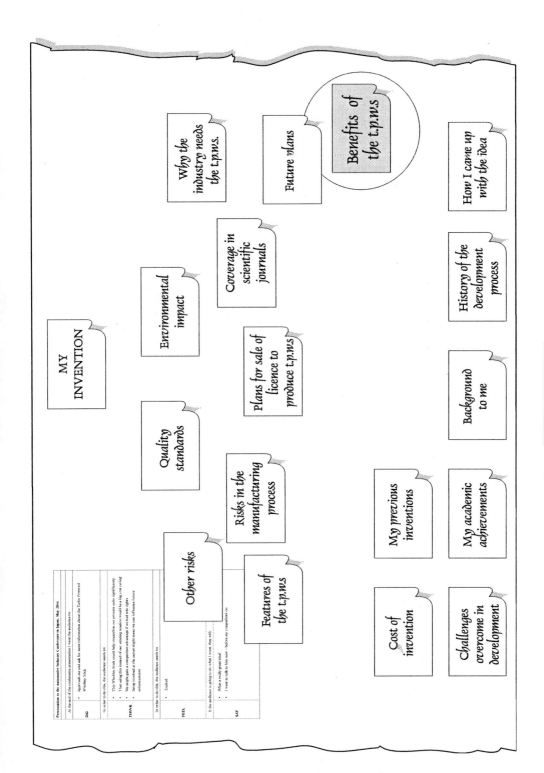

Peter the Project Manager

Peter was working away from home for a few days after he and Chris had finished Stage 3 of the process, so they had a break before coming back to their brown paper and working through Stage 4. As Peter has a very logical and analytical approach he could soon see that several things could actually be left out, as his audience research had helped him to understand that Sarah actually didn't need a lot of the information that he had previously thought. She trusted him to do his job and would ask for more detail if she needed it. Also he recognised that the update meeting was not the right forum to mention a pay rise.

At the end of Stage 4 Peter's brown paper looked like this:

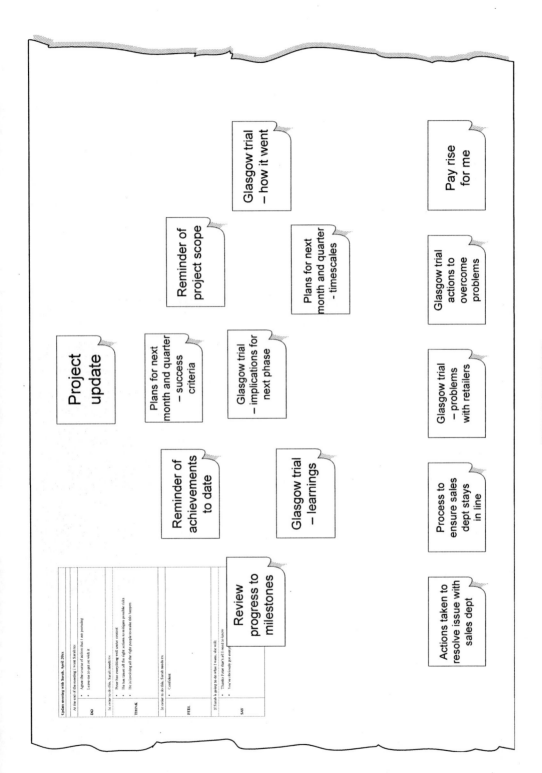

Chrystal and Christof the Creativity Consultants

Mike used the Design Principles Template to remind Chrystal and Christof of what they were aiming to achieve at this meeting. He pointed out that they had spent months dealing with different members of the panel and had given them masses of information in their response to the Invitation to Tender.

He then asked a particularly pertinent question: "Have you been told what the panel want you to focus on in this presentation?" The answer was "yes". They had been asked to focus on how they would work with the Board to ensure the success of the Creativity Programme as this was such a new venture and was seen as high risk.

As a result they decided to miss out much of the background information that they usually included whether it was asked for or not. This meant that there was room to add two topics that they had not even thought about including – 'working with you' and 'tried and trusted approach'.

At the end of Stage 4 their brown paper looked like this:

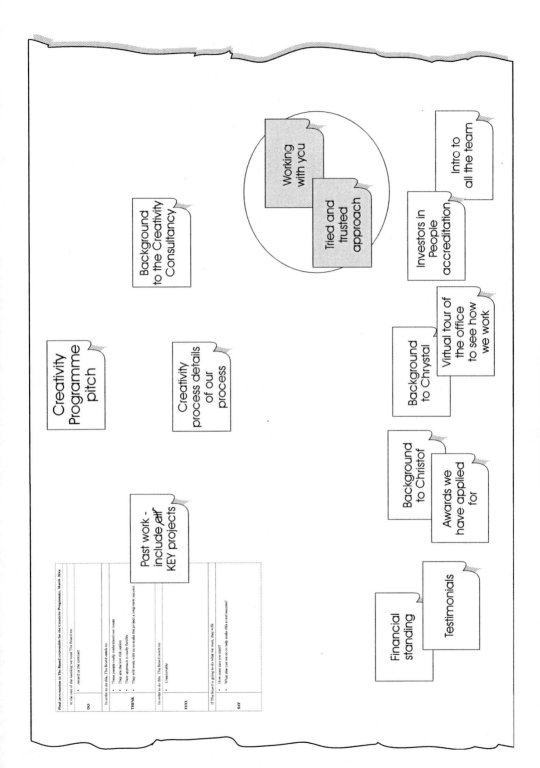

CARVING THE SCULPTURE

BE CLEAR SEVEN STAGE PROCESS™

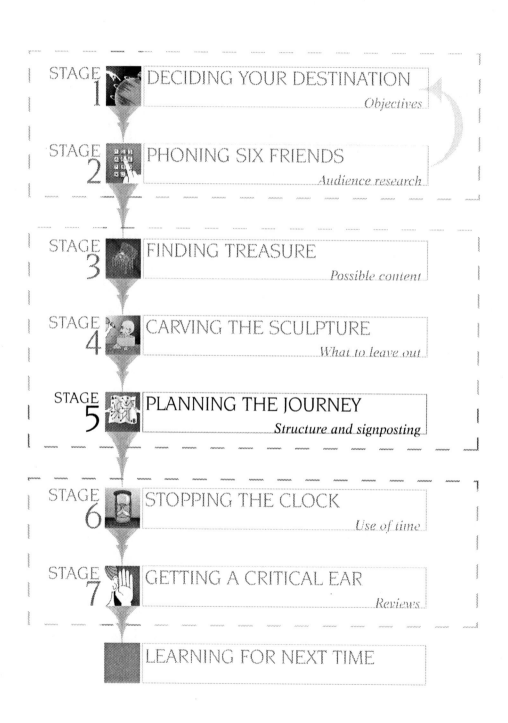

STAGE 1
DECIDING YOUR DESTINATION
Objectives

STAGE 2
PHONING SIX FRIENDS
Audience research

STAGE 3
FINDING TREASURE
Possible content

STAGE 4
CARVING THE SCULPTURE
What to leave out

STAGE 5
PLANNING THE JOURNEY
Structure and signposting

STAGE 6
STOPPING THE CLOCK
Use of time

STAGE 7
GETTING A CRITICAL EAR
Reviews

LEARNING FOR NEXT TIME

PLANNING THE JOURNEY

– 5 –

PLANNING THE JOURNEY   How to take the
content that your audience needs to hear and put it in the best
order for them, ensuring it has a powerful start, a concise
conclusion and clear signposts in between.

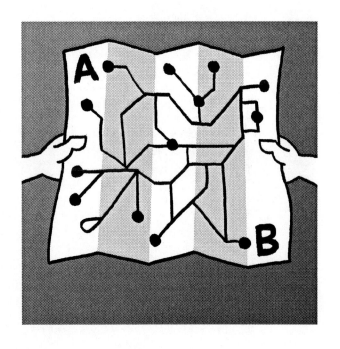

Stage 5

In Chapter 4 – *carving the sculpture* you looked at how to decide what content to include for a specific audience at a particular time, based on your Design Principles. This next stage is all about how you start, how you finish and how you progress from one to the other.

If you have phoned lots of *friends* to research your audience then this stage will be easier. You will have more of an idea of the kind of person or people that you are addressing and what is important to them about your communication.

Within 'planning the journey' you will spend time considering both the structure of your communication and how you signpost that structure for your audience. These are two different but equally important aspects of preparing your communication.

To my mind the two aspects are inextricably linked and hence they are in the same chapter of this book. However, until you have a structure you cannot think of signposts, so they are explained as two separate tools.

The more rigorously you apply Stage 5:

- The more likely you are to put information in the order that the audience needs
- The easier it will be for the audience to understand what you have to say
- Your introductions and conclusions will have more power and impact

Why 'planning the journey' really matters

"He who wishes to talk well must first think well." (Origin unknown)

The use of intentional structure and signposting is the first indication to your audience that this is going to be a particularly clear presentation, rather than just an *average* or *OK* presentation.

Every piece of communication you create will have a structure whether by design or by default. For example, it may be a clearly delineated series of inter-connected short topics beginning with a concise overview and concluding with a summary of the key points. Alternatively, it may be a single mass of information with an unclear starting point that eventually tails off when the speaker runs out of things to say. Aim for the former!

'Planning the journey' can make up for many shortfalls in content. It will immediately make your message more accessible to most business and professional audiences – people who have neither the time nor the inclination for a magical mystery tour through your content.

They want to know when and why they should listen.

Stage 5 is vital because:

- A clear and logical sequence helps the audience to remember your message
- Breaking information into smaller pieces makes it easier for people to understand
- There is always more than one possible way to order your content

The tool – planning your journey

At this point in the process you should have your brown paper in front of you with your chosen content on it. The content is separated into two groups: information to be included in your communication and other information that probably does not apply to this particular meeting or presentation.

The following steps will help you to put that content into the best structure for your audience. As you will see there is always more than one way to order your content!

1 – Break your content into groups of related information

- Look at all the Post-it® notes in the centre of your brown paper and start to put together ones that have a common theme.

- If you do this with a colleague you will probably find that you can each see different ways of grouping some of the information. There is no right or wrong way, only *different* ways.

- Decide between you, which is the right group for this audience at this time.

- Do not worry about how many different groups you have or whether some seem to be sub-sets of others.

2 – Give each group of content a heading

You will be creating a *working heading* at this stage, so it does not need to be fancy or elegant.

- The headings will depend on the content, your audience and how you decide to split that content.

- Use a different colour Post-it® note if you can for your headings – it will help later.

- There is no right or wrong and certainly no magic formula, some examples are shown below:
  - 'what we do', 'why we do it', 'when we do it', 'where we do it', 'how we do it'
  - 'locations', 'alliances and partners', 'people stuff', 'product mix', 'price'
  - 'options', 'resources', 'next steps', 'background', 'sponsorship'.

3 – Break your groups of content into manageable chunks

To do this you need to bear in mind the following principles:

- The human mind likes symmetry and balance. Memory is a complicated thing; help your audience to remember your message by breaking it down into manageable chunks of information of similar size.
- If possible group information into 3s or 5s to give a pyramid structure (shown below).
- If your information logically falls into four areas then use four, however if you end up with six or more areas then you will usually find that your information will fit into sub-groups. So six groups of information could fall into two sub-groups of three, or three sub-groups of two.
- Your brown paper should now be covered with pyramids of Post-it® notes.

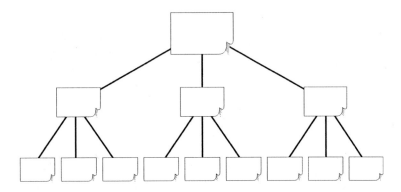

4 – Leave some content in unmanageable chunks, as an exception

You can only get away with using lots of unstructured information (unmanageable chunks) if you want the audience to remember *lots* rather than something *specific*. For example, if you are talking about a business plan that you are preparing and you want your audience to feel that you have been really thorough and considered this from every angle you could give an unstructured list of eight or ten different aspects that you have considered. In this case your audience would be unlikely to remember many of the specific aspects, just *lots*.

5 – Experiment to find the best order for your audience

This is a really important part. Your aim is to break your information down into a pyramid structure, but to do this you need to know the order for the top level of information.

Remind yourself of your audience and what they need to know. Remember they may not be experts on your subject, nor do they need to be. Your aim is to put your information across in a way that is logical for them even if it seems illogical, even alien, to you.

The easy way to do this is to experiment:

- Take all the headings from each of your groups and move to a clear bit of your brown paper or another space.
- Then try *all* the possible different orders in which those headings might go *and* force yourself to talk through how you would link the various parts of the presentation.
- You will find that there is always more than one way to tell your story.

Try moving the heading you would naturally put last and put it first, this is often very powerful. For example, if your final heading is something like 'what we want from you' saying that right at the outset can be very powerful. Busy senior executives tend to appreciate it as they immediately know when and why they need to pay attention.

6 – *Complete your pyramid structure based on the best order for the audience*

- Re-unite the groups of information with the headings to which they relate.
- Now order the groups in the best way for the audience, based on your audience research.

7 – *Use the 1-3-2 rule*

As you make your final adjustments to the structure keep in mind the 'laws of memory' and how they affect the way that you order information.

- Generally people remember what is said at the beginning best, then what is said at the end and then the things that are repeated a lot in the middle.
- Using these laws it makes sense, when you are dealing with topics that are broken into three sub-sections, to put the most important point first, sandwich the least important point in the middle and to put the second most important point at the end.

8 – *Review your pyramid to make sure that it is well balanced*

- Check that you don't have too much information in one area that actually needs to be broken down further into more manageable chunks.
- Look out for anywhere that you have put two small chunks of information next to each other that might be better combined into one topic.

Examples

No surprises

"The problem is that we know this customer is really cost-focused so we need to tell them everything else before we talk about the price."

This is a common comment from sales people and I am inclined to turn it on its head and say that if you know your customer is just waiting to hear the price then tell them it at the outset.

It may seem radical and you may worry that the customer will not listen to anything else, but if that is the case you are probably wasting your time in the first place. Just think of these two scenarios:

Scenario 1 – *The sales person spends twenty minutes giving a slick presentation all about their product including all the wonderful things that it can do and eventually, right at the end, they tell the customer the price.*

Scenario 2 – *The sales person goes into the meeting and says right at the beginning something like: "I know that you are very cost-focused at the moment, so I will cover the price of our product right at the outset. The cost is. . ." After this the sales person goes on to say: "Now I realise that we are not the cheapest in the market and if our price really is outside your budget I'll leave now and not waste any of your time, but I believe that in a few minutes I can show you how the benefits will more than outweigh the capital expenditure. Shall I stay?"*

In the first scenario there is a danger that the audience sits through the whole presentation thinking 'this is all great stuff, but how much does it cost' or even worse 'there's no point me listening as we can't possibly afford something as good as this'. With the second scenario, the customer is likely to be flattered that the presenter has recognised their current focus on costs and has told them what they wanted to hear first, so they can then cut short the meeting (very unlikely) or listen attentively to what the presenter has to say and think about how they can get maximum benefit from the product.

Key point

Forcing your audience to listen to you by leaving the vital information until the end risks alienating them as well as losing their concentration during the presentation.

Tell them why they need to listen

"But she's such a senior executive I wouldn't dream of telling her what I wanted until the end of the meeting."

This is a comment that I often hear when working with people in large organisations who are occasionally asked to present information to people who are more senior than they are. Again let us consider two scenarios:

Scenario 1 *– The person gives a very well-rehearsed presentation about the work that they are undertaking and right at the end comes a plea for some help from the senior executive.*

Scenario 2 – *The person begins by saying: "I am delighted to have the opportunity to present the work our team is undertaking. I hope that as a result you will support our request for / tell other parts of the business about our work / agree to a joint workshop etc."*

In the first scenario the senior executive may be listening to the information patiently and considering it from their point of view. Then at the end they realise something is required of them and so they have to ask for recaps on certain areas because they hadn't been listening out for the information needed to support the request.

With the second scenario your audience knows from the outset what is wanted of them, so they will listen to the information in the context of what they are being asked to do. The other benefit with the second scenario is that they are likely to help the presenter to use the available time more effectively by saying something like: "Well to do that we will need to understand what you are doing to mitigate the risks / involve finance / work alongside the housing department etc."

Remember that senior people rarely have the time or the inclination to go on a *magical mystery tour*, so tell them why you are using some of their valuable time right at the outset.

Key point

Tell your audience what you want from them at the outset, that way they can make an informed decision about what they need to listen to carefully and what is just background information.

Introductions
and conclusions

"You never get a second chance to make a first impression." (Origin unknown)

Now is the time to start considering how you are going to make a good introduction and conclusion for this piece of communication. There are many statistics showing how the first few seconds and minutes are vital as they are the ones in which your audience forms most of their opinion about you and hence, decides whether or not to listen to what you have to say.

Consider the conference presenter who has the slot after lunch. He can either shuffle nervously onto the stage and mumble the few first words of his hesitant introduction, or he can bound onto the stage full of the passion and enthusiasm that he feels for his subject. He has a well-rehearsed attention grabbing introduction that he has prepared to help him transfer all of his passion and enthusiasm to the audience.

But introductions are vital for meetings as well as for formal presentations. Imagine that you are on the panel that is to award a large contract. The short-listed contenders are all presenting to you today.

The current contract holders are sure that they will be successful but even so they have sent a couple of their very senior people in to talk to the panel. These people know several of the panel well and as they enter the room they have an air of confidence that borders on arrogance. They immediately start talking to the people they know, but never actually introduce themselves to you or to the new Head of Purchasing. You are both sitting quietly at the end of the table forming your own fairly negative opinions.

Compare this with the company representatives who enter the room and have a clear leader who introduces each of the team and ensures that they all shake hands and make eye contact with *every* member of the panel before the meeting begins. They also know the importance of a smile!

Appendix 4 gives several ways to grab the audience's attention at the start of your presentation. A copy can be downloaded from http://www.beclear.co.uk/hints.htm.

Introductions should be:

- Well thought through and rehearsed
- Integral to the whole presentation – not just a gimmick
- Engaging, interesting or entertaining for the audience

As well as paying particular attention to your introduction make sure you also have a clear and concise conclusion.

The risk with conclusions is that they are not properly rehearsed, so you end up rambling and the audience is not sure whether you have finished or not. Or you rehearse something but decide during your talk to add something else into your conclusion. The effect will be the same, you will soon be rambling although you may be concentrating so hard on what you are saying that you do not realise that you *lost* most of your audience several minutes before.

Conclusions are important because:

- It is the last thing that your audience hears
- If they have lost concentration a well 'signposted' conclusion will regain their attention
- It is your 'call to action'

A word about 'signposts'

Now that you have 'planned your journey' including giving extra consideration to your introduction and conclusion, you need to think about how to share that plan with your audience so that they know what to expect. To do this you need to 'signpost' your communication.

Signposting is a fundamental tool for both spoken and written communication. In written business communication signposts are often applied almost without conscious thought through the use of headings, paragraphs and section breaks. All these help the reader to see the context of the document, as well as showing the flow of information and highlighting when we are moving to another theme.

Signposts in presentations are often much more subtle and sometimes people forget them altogether. As an example someone might say: "I'll start with financial, move onto technical and finish with the benefits." Then, as the speaker progresses through the talk, he will say: "So, now I have covered the financial aspects I will move onto the second section, technical." At the end of the technical section the speaker will verbally signpost that they are going onto the third part, the benefits.

To my mind, signposts are even more important with verbal communication than they are with written. Here are just three of the reasons why:

- **Signposts provide context** – signposting at the beginning of any communication helps your audience to prepare their mind to receive information. Anyone who has trained to improve their reading speed, will know the importance of flicking through a document and reading the various headings before diving into the first paragraph. If the presenter gives an overview of the topics the audience's minds are similarly well prepared.

- **Signposts help the audience re-engage** – if your audience loses concentration when reading your document they will tend to go back to the last heading and re-read from there. With a presentation it is difficult (not to mention embarrassing) for your audience to ask you to go back to the place where they lost concentration! Remember, however engaging your delivery, the audience will not listen all the time, in fact some statistics suggest they will lose concentration as often as every 90 seconds. If you verbally signpost moving to a new section it is easy for them to re-engage.

- **Signposts guide mixed audiences** – when you address an audience of more than one person you have the added complication that different people are interested in different parts of your talk, have different levels of knowledge and listen in different ways. Signposting helps them pay particular attention to the most relevant parts for them.

The more formal the presentation the more important it is to have good signposting. It is still important in meetings, but will tend to be obvious as the host or chairperson moves through the agenda.

'Signposts' are vital because:

- They help your audience to prepare for what they are about to hear
- Telling your audience where you are in the sequence reassures them and means that they listen to the parts that are most relevant to them
- They help the speaker to stay on track and not wander off at a tangent

The tool – signposts

The steps for this tool may look small, but this is one of those situations where a small amount of effort can reap great rewards. Applying these three steps can add a great deal to your presentation.

1 – Review your structure and decide on the level of signposting appropriate to your audience

If your audience knows you and your subject, they may need less signposting than those who do not. But bear in mind if they have a lot of other calls on their time, remembering the specifics of your project may not be high on their agenda.

2 – Consider whether your working headings will be suitable for the audience

A jokey, fun or slang term such as 'financial stuff' or 'the numbers' might work for a group of young designers, but you probably need something more serious for a meeting with city financiers. As always think of your audience.

PLANNING THE JOURNEY

3 – *Work out the links you will make as you move from section to section*

Decide how you will signpost the end of one section and the start of the next, as well as the sub-sections within them. The three key principles to remember are:

- **Signpost where you are going** – "Ladies and gentlemen I am going to tell you about . . . to do so we will look at three areas: firstly . . . ; then secondly we will consider . . . ; finally we will look at . . ."

- **Signpost the end of each section** – "So that is all I want to cover in terms of . . . and to recap on this section, the main points are . . ."

- **Signpost the start of a new section** – "Now in the second section of my presentation, we will be considering . . . in particular . . . "

The exact words will change according to your personal style and the content of your presentation. However, if you rehearse your signposts when you rehearse your presentation you will soon have clear signposts for your audience that are an integral part of your presentation and help to keep you on track!

Making 'planning the journey' work for you

There can seem to be a lot to think about when you are first applying these principles, so remember the key things about Stage 5 are:

- **More complicated messages need more structure** – the more you break it down into smaller more manageable chunks the easier it is to understand.

- **'3s and 5s' are ideal but '2s and 4s' are OK** – breaking your content into smaller sections helps the audience to store the information in their memory.

- **Lots of unstructured content will be remembered as 'lots'** – this *should only be used* if you want people to have an overall impression rather than remembering specifics.

- **Your opening and closing words are vital** – these are the parts that your audience listen to and remember the most.

- **Signpost where you are going** – help your audience to mentally prepare for what is coming next, to pay particular attention to the key parts for them and to re-engage when they lose concentration.

No time for 'planning the journey'

If you have made the time for *deciding your destination, phoning six friends, finding treasure and carving the sculpture* this part is really quick and easy. However, if as often happens you succumb to the temptation to dive straight into structuring your content before doing everything else first you will usually find yourself going round and round in circles.

The most common thing people say to me is: "I didn't think I had time to work out what I needed the audience to **think, feel, say** and **do** . . . I thought I knew what I wanted to achieve . . . but then I got in a real mess and couldn't figure out what to include or what to leave out . . . so eventually, I decided it might help to think a bit about the objectives . . . suddenly it all fell into place . . . I'll always do it at the outset from now on, no matter how little time I have!"

Having spent time 'planning the journey' your 'signposts' will easily fall into place, the important thing is to spend some time rehearsing them if you do not usually use this method of helping your audience to follow what you are saying.

If you really are short of time for 'planning your journey':

- Quickly group your information and give each group a heading – remember to use '3s and 5s' if possible
- Put the titles in three or four different orders – particularly try moving the content you would naturally put at the end to the beginning
- Spend time thinking about your opening and closing words – these are vital, use them wisely

What next?

By now you have decided what content to include and have put it in a great order that matches the needs of the audience. You should also recognise how important it is to research your audience at the outset. Their age, gender, passions and interests as well as whether they are task or people orientated will all influence the way in which you structure your communication.

Now, go on to Chapter 6 – *stopping the clock* to discover different ways to use the time available and to see how this can vary depending on your audience and what you are trying to achieve.

CASE STUDIES – STAGE 5

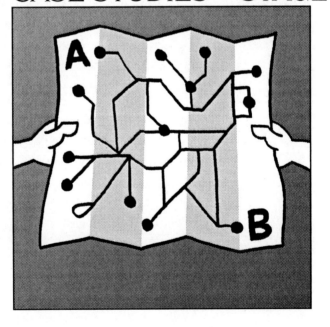

Boffin the Inventor

As soon as Boffin, Igor and Sally had completed Stage 4 they went onto Stage 5. They were all quickly in agreement about how to group the main pieces of information. However they had quite strong disagreements about the order that the groups should be put in.

Sally and Igor both said that Boffin needed to start with the benefits that the Turbo Powered Wimbley Stick offered over the existing Steam Powered Wimbley Stick and in the face of united opposition Boffin agreed. He kept saying that it wasn't logical to him, he wanted to start with 'quality', or ideally 'history' but he had been persuaded to take that part out in Stage 4. Both Igor and Sally said it would be logical to his audience to start with benefits and eventually he accepted their arguments as he freely admitted they had far more commercial acumen than him.

They all agreed that Boffin would need to spend some time rehearsing giving the information in the new order, together with its signposts as he is in the habit of explaining everything chronologically without any obvious breaks or sections.

At the end of Stage 5 their brown paper looked like this:

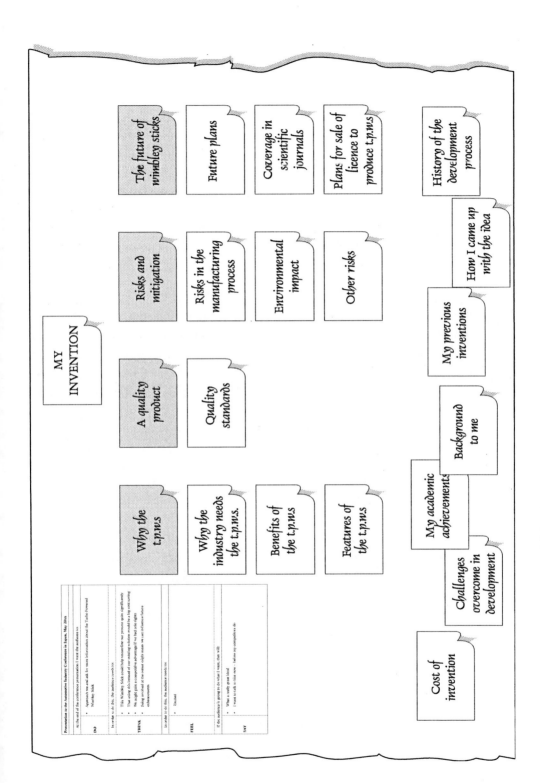

Peter the Project Manager

Peter spent some time looking at the information that he had gleaned from his 'friends' before he grouped his content and tried to put it in different orders.

Logic said to him that he should begin with a review of progress against all the project milestones but his audience research told him that Sarah would be really interested in what happened in Glasgow. Even more than that she would be particularly interested in any implications for future trials and the plans for roll-out.

So he tried putting Glasgow first and highlighted in the heading that he was going to focus on the implications for other work. With the benefit of his audience research he could now see that when Sarah had gone off at tangents in the past it was usually because she was considering how the learning from one project could be applied to others. He just hadn't realised it before.

Now it seemed quite logical to talk about Glasgow first, particularly as it was by far the most important part of his work.

At the end of Stage 5 Peter's brown paper looked like this:

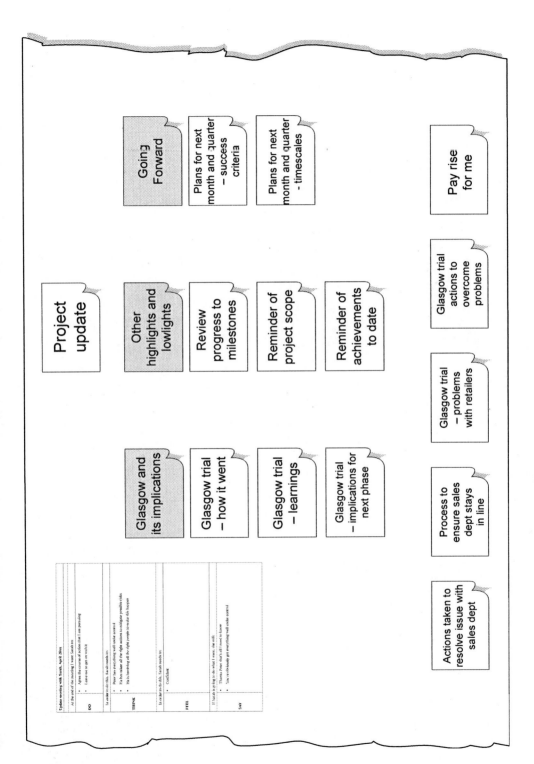

Chrystal and Christof the Creativity Consultants

Now that Mike knew about the importance of safety and a low risk approach, he helped Chrystal and Christof to see that much of the information they were putting over needed to highlight how they were the low risk option.

As a result they put in a whole new section on 'partnership working' and the section on 'creativity' which included key projects they had worked on in the past would now highlight how they introduced creativity in a variety of situations whilst managing the process to negate risk as far as possible.

Chrystal felt there was a risk they wouldn't show off their incredible creative brilliance to maximum effect, but Christof could see that in the past it was the presentations that had really exhibited their creative flair to the full that had been the ones where they had failed. He thought maybe the potential customers just weren't ready for everything that they could do for them, and they needed to introduce their ideas more gradually as people began to trust them.

Also they agreed to put the part about The Creativity Consultancy in the middle rather than at the outset, so that they could start with what mattered most to the potential client.

The end result was a brown paper that looked like this:

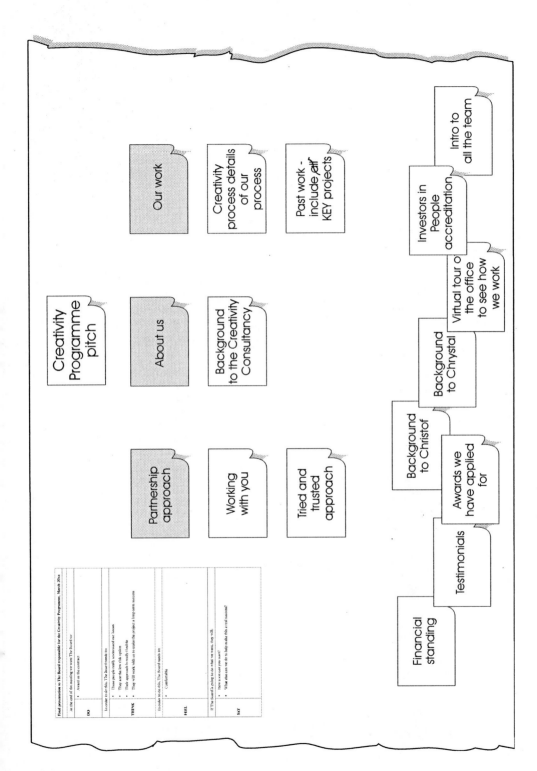

BE CLEAR SEVEN STAGE PROCESS

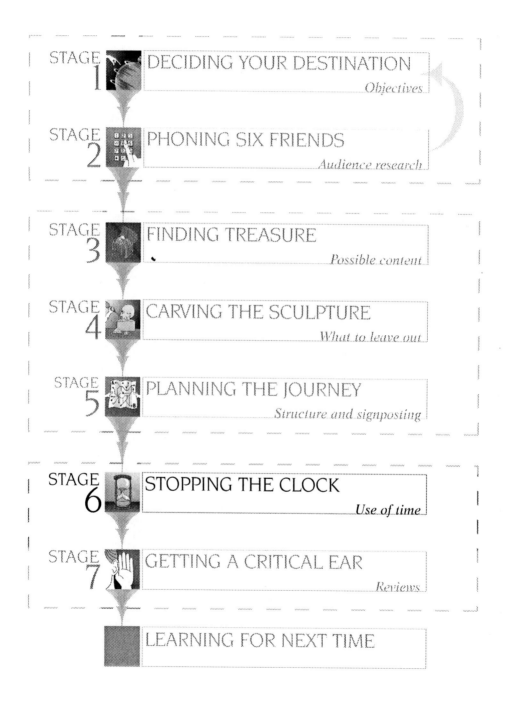

STAGE
1 — DECIDING YOUR DESTINATION
Objectives

STAGE
2 — PHONING SIX FRIENDS
Audience research

STAGE
3 — FINDING TREASURE
Possible content

STAGE
4 — CARVING THE SCULPTURE
What to leave out

STAGE
5 — PLANNING THE JOURNEY
Structure and signposting

STAGE
6 — STOPPING THE CLOCK
Use of time

STAGE
7 — GETTING A CRITICAL EAR
Reviews

LEARNING FOR NEXT TIME

– 6 –

STOPPING THE CLOCK How to use the time
you have available in the most effective and varied way while
enhancing your credibility.

Stage 6

By now you have considered your audience, where you want to take them and the information that you need to take them there. In Chapter 6 – *stopping the clock* you will learn how to consider the time you have available so that you use each valuable minute and second to your advantage.

Time is something that many people never even consider. I hear people say things like: "the conference organiser said I had thirty minutes so I padded out my presentation to fill it," or "we always present for 45 minutes and leave 15 minutes for questions and answers." My response, as you can probably guess, is along the lines of "but is that the best use of time for your audience?"

This chapter will show you why you should question these types of assumptions. In addition it will give you three key principles to consider when you are 'stopping the clock' so that you use the time you have to maximum effect.

Thinking more about the time you have available will mean that you can:

- Be far more in control of any meeting or presentation
- Give back excess time that you do not need
- Use a variety of styles to maximise the time available

Why 'stopping the clock' really matters

"Time and tide wait for no man"
(Origin unknown)

This stage is important because time is the most precious commodity that you have when you are face-to-face with people so you must use it wisely.

Remember, you are responsible for your audience's time as well as your own. If you waffle for 10 minutes at a conference when speaking to 500 people, you have wasted more than 10 minutes of your own time. You have also wasted 5,000 minutes or 83.5 hours of the audience's time.

Asking for a shorter speaking slot is something people often don't consider, but can have many advantages:

- You speak for the right amount of time to cover your subject matter.
- Your audience is far less likely to become bored. After all you don't need to 'pad it out a bit'.
- The conference organiser can allow time for over-runs as well as adding a few minutes onto lunch or coffee.
- The conference programme will have more interest and variety with people speaking for different lengths of time.

Of course there may be occasions when you really need more than the time that has been allotted to you and if one of the other speakers has said they do not need all the time that has been given to them, you may be able to extend your slot.

Use of time is equally important in a one-to-one meeting. It is not unknown for people to start with the less important issues and then to run out of time for the more important issues or to have to rush them, as they had under-estimated how long the other points might take. If the item gets moved to the next meeting agenda in a month or six-weeks' time that can have serious implications.

Stage 6 is vital because:

- You are responsible for both your own and the audience's time
- Different audiences like time to be used in different ways
- Changing the ratio of presenting to discussing can affect the outcome of the intervention

The tool –
stopping the
clock

There is no magic here. It is simply down to your audience research. The more you know about the audience, the more likely you are to recognise the most effective way to use the time you have with them.

Knowing what you do about the audience, you can apply the following three simple principles to any meeting or presentation to decide on the best use of time. They do not all apply to every situation, but many of them apply to more than one. Single Point Communication is so varied that it is impossible to be more specific.

The three key principles are:

- Interaction is good
- Spontaneity builds credibility
- Present first

These principles are examined in more detail below. They are then discussed in terms of the three Case Studies at the end of the chapter.

Interaction is good

When you give information and there is little or no opportunity for feedback from the audience (say, for example, at a formal presentation when you would be telling the audience what you think they want to hear), then no matter how good your audience research may be you will never know for certain what they actually want to hear.

Yet in more interactive presentations, when you respond to requests for information and questions from the audience you are giving them information that is definitely of interest to them.

When you are giving a formal presentation and you do not have the opportunity for audience interaction, then it is wise to keep your presentation as short as possible. Most business presentations should last no more than 20 minutes without some audience interaction or introspection. If your presentation needs to last longer than 20 minutes, think about how you can keep the interest going and hang onto their attention. One method might be to split your presentation into sections and to take questions half way through or at the end of each section of your presentation. Alternatively you could ask rhetorical questions, which give the impression of audience interaction and let them think about themselves for a moment, yet without breaking the flow. The important thing here is to consider what may be best for your audience while remaining aware that there are some options available to you.

STOPPING THE CLOCK

If you are presenting to a small group of people or just one person, then you can involve your audience by outlining the topic areas that you are planning to cover at the outset. You can then ask two or three short questions to involve them in the agenda. For example:

- Which of the topics are of most interest to you?
- Are there any other topics you would like me to cover?
- Are there any that you would prefer me to leave out?

If you present your topics as a spider diagram (shown below) with space for the audience to add topics you will find that you immediately engage them. Also, you end up with a flexible agenda, to which you can keep drawing them back if they start to divert into other issues. In doing this you are also showing that you are confident enough in your subject to allow them to add in topics and alter the order in which you may have planned to speak.

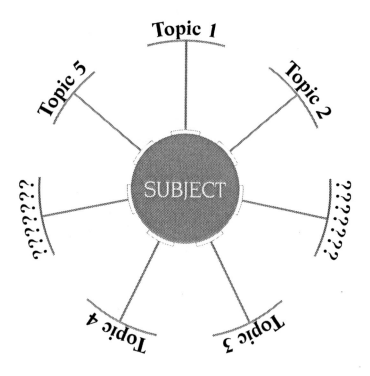

Spontaneity builds credibility

"I'm just preparing my impromptu remarks."
(Winston Churchill)

Anyone can learn a script. Only an expert can answer questions under pressure confidently and fluently. This means that when you are speaking in a formal presentation or even an informal one where you are primarily imparting information that you have prepared in advance, you will have less credibility than when you are responding to your audience's questions and observations.

As an example, any of my clients could develop a presentation with me and help me to prepare a word-perfect script. I could rehearse this until I delivered it as though I were the world's greatest expert on the subject. All would be well until one of the audience asked a question, at that point my lack of knowledge would be immediately evident.

Where speakers positively encourage questions and where bid teams positively encourage discussion it usually means that they have rehearsed answers to all the likely questions so that they have little to fear from the audience, in fact they positively relish the opportunity to show how well prepared they are.

At the end of this section there is the step-by-step process that I use when helping clients to prepare for audience questions whether it is a conference speech, a one-to-one meeting or a competitive bid situation.

Present first

Set the standard for the other presenters to meet by taking the opportunity to present first wherever possible. Similarly try to submit documents slightly ahead of the deadline so that yours is read first.

STOPPING THE CLOCK

So why present first? Because the first response usually sets the standard for the rest – this is assuming that it is of a reasonable standard.

The following sweepingly stereotypical example is given without apology, as it is so often true and most people can relate to it . . .

The time of the Christmas Party is fast approaching and it is time for Jess to buy a new frock. Her long suffering partner Jim is dragged along into town on a Saturday morning, on an urgent mission with Jess, who cannot possibly wear the same outfit that she wore last year.

Jess and Jim go into the first store and find a very nice frock, but Jess just wants to try a few more shops before making up her mind (does this sound familiar?). Many hours later and with sore and aching feet, Jess and Jim make their way back to the first store and buy the first dress that Jess tried on.

I am sure you can think of other examples, where after much searching you go back to the one you saw first.

In these cases the first thing you saw provided an acceptable solution; when you look at anything else it will have to appear significantly better before you will buy that in preference to the first. Also the laws of memory show us that people remember the first thing the best.

Some of you may now be thinking that appearing last is the next best time to present. However, from my own experience of being on the panel at a *beauty parade* for awarding a large contract, I can honestly say that by the time you get to the last presentation, you really just want it to be over. This is in no way the fault of the presenters, it is just that by the end you have heard several companies all telling you about their achingly similar products or services. Whilst the bidders can see significant differences in their offerings, to the buyers most of them will be pretty much the same.

So if you can, ask to present first.

Rehearsing the Q&A session

"What do you mean – rehearse the Question & Answer session?"

New clients often ask this question in a tone of near incredulity – particularly when I say that it can take half a day or more to prepare adequately.

A great deal of attention goes into crafting an excellent presentation. The problem is that the audience, usually a panel of several people, want to hear your answers to their questions. They may be thinking of awkward questions or *curved balls* that they can use to catch you out.

So how do you avoid being *on the back foot* either literally or metaphorically?

1 – *Brainstorm with your colleagues a list of at least 50 questions that you could be asked*

- Include the silly ones and the ones people could only ask if they hadn't listened attentively to the presentation.

2 – *Ask someone who won't be at the meeting to fire the questions at the team*

- I use the word *fire*, because this should be quick and snappy to make sure you know who is going to answer each type of question.

3 – *Answer the questions out loud*

- Speaking the answers out loud helps in two ways: firstly, it forces the person answering to think right though the answer; secondly, colleagues can suggest ways to improve the answer.

4 – *Go over the answers to questions that you are uncomfortable with or which highlight your weaknesses*

- Strong, well thought through answers to these are likely to win the business.

5 – *Keep the list and add to it after every* **beauty parade** *or meeting*

- It will be a useful reminder for experienced team members and an invaluable aid to those attending for the first time.
- Remember the answers that apply will be different for different audiences – so you need to rehearse the Q&A for every single pitch.

Making 'stopping the clock' work for you

The key things to remember about Stage 6 are:

- **Higher levels of interaction are best, but need more preparation** – the more interaction there is between you and the audience the more chance you have of giving the right information to move the audience forward.
- **'Off the cuff' remarks and apparently spontaneous answers have more credibility, but they need to be rehearsed** – given time, anyone can learn a speech. It takes an expert to answer probing questions confidently and fluently or to know when to admit that they do not know the answer.

- **Use as much time as you need and no more** – give the extra time back, no-one complains if a meeting finishes early, but someone will if it finishes late.

This is also a good time to consider what you will do if your allotted time is halved or doubled. It is easy to work out your strategy at this point in your planning; it can be a nightmare if you are told five minutes before you begin that your 30-minute slot has been cut in half and suddenly you need to decide how to cut your material.

No time for 'stopping the clock'

The concept of not having time to consider how to use time has a certain irony to it!

I know from my work with clients over many years that this step only takes a matter of minutes to consider. Once you are aware of these principles you will begin thinking of them automatically when you are preparing for meetings and presentations. You will also think about how other people use time when they are presenting to or meeting with you.

Once you have read this chapter you will know the three principles, depending on how much time you have available will depend on how much you can prepare yourself so that higher levels of interaction and spontaneity can still be achieved without increasing the risk of you losing control or credibility.

What next?

Well you are almost there! All you need to do now is go on to the final chapter, Chapter 7 – *getting a critical ear.* Read on to find out about getting someone to review your presentation.

Hopefully you will have done this as you have been going through the process, but now is the single most important time to get an external opinion.

Once you have spent time with your reviewer you can begin polishing your presentation, preparing your visual aids and rehearsing your delivery.

CASE STUDIES – STAGE 6

Boffin the Inventor

Situation: The conference organiser has told Boffin that he has a 40-minute slot immediately after lunch. Questions are to be to a panel of all the afternoon speakers together.

Boffin has spent sometime with Igor thinking about the way that he can use the time available, they have come up with three options:

1 – Speak for the full 40 minutes without any audience interaction.

2 – Speak for 15 minutes, have 10 minutes of participation and interaction from the audience, and then speak for another 15 minutes.

3 – Speak for 15 minutes and have 15 minutes for questions and answers, give 10 minutes back to the conference organiser

Advantages and disadvantages of the options

Unless Boffin is an outstanding speaker, which he is not, Option 1 is a non-starter. Igor explains to Boffin that even an outstanding speaker would only make it work by having high-levels of audience interest and involvement.

Forty minutes is a very long time for people to just sit and listen, especially immediately after lunch when they may be feeling more than a little soporific. Depending on Boffin's invention there may be ways that he can involve the audience but as he is not a very confident speaker this would be quite high risk.

Boffin's other alternatives are to reduce the length of his speaking slot and either have a Question & Answer session in his own speaking slot, or tell the organiser he does not need so much time.

He would prefer to have more time for audience questions as he is very knowledgeable about his subject and decides to speak to the conference organiser about whether this would be possible. Assuming that the technology is available in terms of roving microphones and so on then this is probably the best solution for Boffin.

Igor says that he and Sarah will help come up with a long list of possible questions and will rehearse with Boffin until he can answer every one of them, including the ones about his previous inventions and their lack of commercial success – in other words the questions Boffin hates.

STOPPING THE CLOCK

Peter the Project Manager

Situation: Peter is meeting his boss Sarah for their monthly project update. The meeting is scheduled for 30 minutes, but is often shortened as Sarah is so busy. Peter is uncomfortable presenting because Sarah often goes off at tangents.

Peter has talked to his partner Chris about the various ways that he could use the time available. They have considered three options:

1 –   Prepare a presentation with slides on a laptop that will take about 20 minutes to present and allow 10 minutes of questions at the end. This is Peter's usual method.

2 –   Prepare all the information that Peter thinks he may need to cover, take in a spider diagram as a suggestion of possible topic areas and invite Sarah to decide which areas to cover first.

3 –   Prepare a 5-minute presentation of the key changes since the last meeting and use this as a springboard for discussion.

Advantages and disadvantages of the options

Peter prefers Option 1 and this is the way he normally presents to Sarah. It is his way of trying to keep Sarah on track though it hardly ever works! Thanks to the time Peter has spent *phoning six friends* he now realises that this is probably not the best way to present to Sarah. He now knows that she likes to have more control and is only interested in hearing about what has happened as a way of influencing what will happen in the future.

Options 2 and 3 are ones that Peter has never considered before. He is more than a little uncomfortable with such an unstructured meeting. In reality though both these options would leave Peter more in control. Chris points out that he would have time to answer Sarah's questions without simultaneously panicking about all the other information that he has decided she needs to hear – whether she listens or not!

Also Peter is now including much less information in his update, so he should be able to explain things at a more leisurely pace and reinforce the key messages as appropriate. He decides that he will try Option 2, but only after he has spoken to another couple of his 'friends' to check that they agree that it should work.

STOPPING THE CLOCK

Chrystal and Christof the Creativity Consultants

Situation: Chrystal and Christof are presenting to a panel of four people. The meeting is scheduled to last two hours and all three short-listed bidders are being seen in one day.

Mike has spent some time with Chrystal and Christof considering different ways they can use the two-hour slot that they have. The options they considered are:

1 –   Prepare a presentation lasting 1.5 hours giving each of them roughly 45 minutes to present and leaving 30 minutes for questions and answers at the end.

2 – Prepare a really short and succinct presentation lasting 15 – 20 minutes given by the most dynamic presenter and allow the rest of the time for answering questions.

3 – Prepare a 15 or 20-minute presentation for Chrystal and another one of similar length for Christof with questions at the end of each, breaking the two hours into two parts, one section on creativity and the other about how the project would happen in practice.

They also spent a few moments discussing whether they can bring their presentation forward so that they are seen first. However, Christof admits that he asked for them to present last so that they would have as much time as possible to prepare. In the circumstances, he cannot really go back to his contact and ask to present first, but he knows what to do next time.

be clear

Advantages and disadvantages of the options

Most audiences have very short attention spans, even with good structure and signposting you should limit the length of any one person's presentation to 15 – 20 minutes at the most. Two successive speakers each lasting 45 minutes is likely to become very boring, very quickly. This is particularly so in a case like this as the audience must know everything there is to know about the bid by now. Restating it all . . . or worse, trying to condense hundreds of pages of bid submission into 90 minutes of verbal presentation is a recipe for disaster.

Mike's work with them so far has helped Chrystal and Christof to see the presentation from their audience's point of view so they no longer want to consider Option 1.

Option 3 would enable them to break the presentation time with interaction in the form of questions, however realising that the panel are seeing them at the end of a long day, they agree with Mike that a short and succinct presentation is now more important than ever.

They decide to give a really short and snappy presentation of the top three reasons for working with the Creativity Consultancy – that is from the panel's point of view.

After the short presentation, they will invite the panel to ask anything at all that they want to know more about. They will also ask them to voice any little niggling concerns that they may have left. If all the questions are finished in 30 minutes, then Christof will ask for the business and they will *leave*.

If they finish early the audience will usually be delighted – they will have thought about the audience's needs, given them as much opportunity to ask questions as possible and left them with an hour to catch up on their e-mails or surprise their partners by arriving home early!

STOPPING THE CLOCK

BE CLEAR SEVEN STAGE PROCESS™

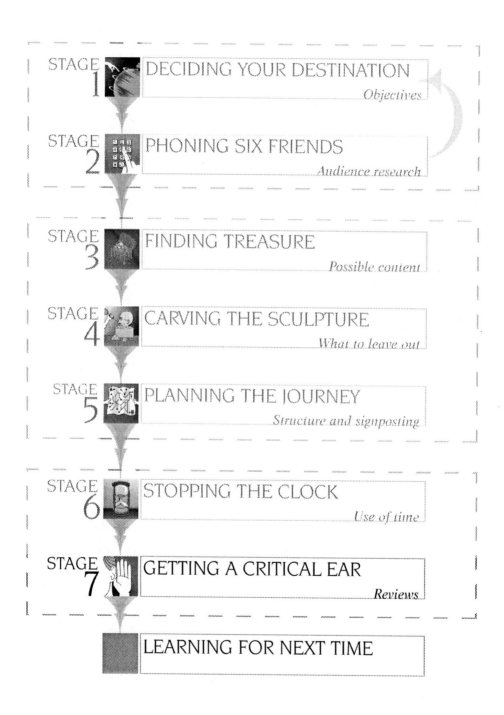

STAGE 1 — DECIDING YOUR DESTINATION
Objectives

STAGE 2 — PHONING SIX FRIENDS
Audience research

STAGE 3 — FINDING TREASURE
Possible content

STAGE 4 — CARVING THE SCULPTURE
What to leave out

STAGE 5 — PLANNING THE JOURNEY
Structure and signposting

STAGE 6 — STOPPING THE CLOCK
Use of time

STAGE 7 — GETTING A CRITICAL EAR
Reviews

LEARNING FOR NEXT TIME

GETTING A CRITICAL EAR

− 7 −

GETTING A CRITICAL EAR How to get the
most from time spent with an external reviewer and how to add
real value if you are the reviewer.

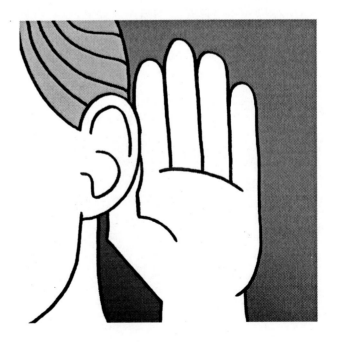

Stage 7

Once you get to this stage in your preparation, it is vital to get another person's opinion before you start spending time enriching stories, learning your introduction and developing visual aids, not to mention preparing any memory prompts and rehearsing your presentation.

Getting an honest opinion from a third party is crucial. You might ask someone related to your work such as your boss, or a colleague. Or you could ask someone entirely unrelated such as your partner, a friend or a member of your family.

There are several times in the overall process when getting a third party's opinion is helpful and these are summarised in this chapter. I also provide guidance that will help you to elicit valuable, constructive feedback every time you get 'a critical ear'.

If there is one person who certainly cannot provide *a critical ear* then it is you! Do not kid yourself that you can. Feedback can only be provided by a third party – whether they have knowledge of your subject or not.

Spending time on this stage helps you:

* To experience the message as your audience will
* To learn from another person's experience
* To experiment with new ideas in a safe environment

Why 'getting
a critical ear'
really matters

"I not only use all the brains I have, but all I can borrow." (Woodrow Wilson)

No two people will ever have exactly the same point of view, because we are all so gloriously different.

The most valuable external reviews usually come from people who know nothing about the subject or who have very different personality types from your own. They may question your most fundamental beliefs, so this is another time when it helps to leave your ego at home.

The reviewer may say many things that you disagree with. Furthermore, their lack of knowledge may mean that they ask *ridiculous* questions. However, for each question that you can dismiss easily there will probably be another that is priceless in helping you to appreciate how different audiences may receive your message.

If you only have time for one review, this is the time to do it.

Stage 7 is vital because:

• As the expert you are 'too close' to the subject

• Every person will interpret your message differently

• The more you understand how your message can be received, the more likely you are to give it in the right way

GETTING A CRITICAL EAR

The tool – getting a critical ear

Ideally you should have two reviewers, one who knows the subject quite well and one who knows little or nothing about your subject. The best thing is to get together with both of your reviewers and anyone who has worked closely with you during the preparation and set aside some time to spend together. In this way you will be able to discuss the implications of changes that anyone suggests.

Go through the following steps with your reviewers:

1 – Give the reviewers the Design Principles

- The **audience research** part will help them to get into the audience's frame of mind.
- The **objectives** point to what the reviewers should check for as you talk through your presentation or meeting plan.

2 – Give your presentation or talk through your meeting plan

- As far as possible, you should do this as though the reviewers are the actual audience. It might as well be your first rehearsal.

3 – Ask your reviewers three critical questions:

- Given my audience research, if you were the audience, would the presentation or meeting make you **think, feel, say** and **do** the things I want the audience to **think, feel, say** and **do**? If so **why**?
- What else does it make you **think, feel, say** and **do**?
- What else could I do that might possibly improve the communication for this particular audience at this point in time?

These three questions are vital, so let's consider them in a little more detail.

Would it make you think, feel, say and do the things I want the audience to think, feel, say and do?

This is the most important question and you need your reviewers to give you more than a simple 'yes' or 'no'. You need to know which parts of the presentation or meeting achieved those objectives and why.

The insights the answers provide will help you not only with this piece of communication, but with every future presentation you give, or meeting you run as you will gain a better understanding of how people interpret your message.

What else does it make you think, feel, say and do?

Whilst you are planning the various messages that you want the audience to receive, you will almost certainly include other messages that might be helpful. At the same time some of them may be unhelpful. Knowing what else you may be inadvertently communicating is very important. When your reviewers tell you what they think, your instinctive response may be to say: "but I didn't mean you to **think** or **feel** that!" However, your reaction should be to acknowledge what they say and to do something about it. You may decide that it is helpful to include this inadvertent message, at other times you may not. The key thing to remember is that you do not want to risk confusing your audience if you can possibly help it.

What you mean the audience to **think** and **feel**, and what they actually **think** and **feel** are often very different. A really good presenter works tirelessly to reduce the gap between the two. The only way to do so is through constant reviews of the effectiveness of their communication both during the

GETTING A CRITICAL EAR

preparation stages (the questions I am outlining now) and after the event (a process I will outline later in this chapter).

What else could I do that might possibly improve the communication for this particular audience at this point in time?

This question is phrased deliberately to encourage your reviewers to give you lots of ideas of things you could *possibly* do to improve. If they give you five ideas and one of them will help to significantly improve the presentation or meeting then you have a good outcome.

There is a checklist of things for your reviewers to consider in Appendix 5. A copy can be downloaded from http://www. beclear.co.uk/hints.htm.

Other times for 'getting a critical ear'

There are three other review points that are key:

- **At the end of Stage 2** – your objectives and audience research are the foundation for your communication, before you spend time considering your content and structure it is important to get an external view of the first two stages if you can.

- **At the dress rehearsal** – there should be no need for fundamental changes here, but 'a critical ear' can suggest fine tuning and subtle changes in emphasis that can help hugely. Remember to include a rehearsal of answers to difficult questions and to rehearse in half the expected time (see Chapter 6 – *stopping the clock*).

- **After the event** – if you want to improve for the future, this review is vital. It is best to use a third party to facilitate the review for you even if you presented as part of a team. Your facilitator should guide you and prompt you through the following questions:

- Did the audience **think, feel, say** and **do** what we wanted them to **think, feel, say** and **do** – what evidence was there?
- What went well?
- What didn't go well / as planned?
- What could we possibly have done differently?

Going through these questions will give you a good record of things to build on and improve for next time.

There is a copy of a template giving these questions in Appendix 6. A copy can be downloaded from http://www.beclear.co.uk/hints.htm.

Examples

What is the audience expecting?

"Your presentation matches your objectives really well, but it doesn't seem to match the conference billing . . . "

This is what I had to say to a brand new client at our first meeting!

The arrangement to speak at the conference had been made months before by the company's marketing department. In the intervening months Paul had remembered the title that had been agreed, but he hadn't looked at the more detailed bullet points outlining the key points of his talk.

My bombshell comment came just a couple of days before the conference. We spent a couple of hours looking critically at the content – it included all the key points listed in the billing, but not in a way that would meet the audience's expectations.

Luckily, Paul knew his subject really well, so we managed to re-structure the presentation to meet the conference billing and leave him time for a thorough rehearsal of the new introduction, signposting and conclusion.

Changing the structure really mattered because whilst some of the audience would not have read the billing, others certainly would. The people who had read it would have an expectation that would have made Paul's presentation difficult to follow and would probably have left them feeling disappointed.

Key point

Your reviewer should take an holistic approach and think of the audience's expectations when they receive your message. They must also be brave enough to tell you things that you may not wish to hear.

Are you slipping into jargon?

"Do all your clients understand what XYZ stands for?" I asked.

"No, that's why we don't use it in sales meetings or presentations," said the client.

This exchange took place after my client, Anne, had talked through their corporate credentials presentation. She was adamant that she hadn't used the abbreviation, but I pointed out that she must have done, because it was the first time I had heard the term.

Two of her colleagues were with us and all of them soon recognised how easily they slipped into jargon and abbreviations without even realising it. This often happens when people are feeling under pressure; times like formal presentations and sales meetings – you have been warned!

Key point

Your reviewer should make the run through as realistic as possible including being quite hostile to put you under pressure. You should also think of how you will enter the room, or walk on to the stage.

Do the key messages really stand out?

"Do all the firms who are after this contract have industry accredited staff?" I asked.

"No, that's why we make such a big thing of it," *said the client.*

As you have probably guessed, it didn't come across as a key message to me.

In fact, when Jason mentioned that all their employees were industry accredited he said it as the third point in the fifth section of his presentation. It sounded vaguely interesting, but it wasn't positioned as a winning point of difference. It transpired that it had originally been in the introduction, but because there was so much information that Jason and his co-directors were trying to include in the presentation, it had been moved a few times, until it was in danger of being buried in detail.

GETTING A CRITICAL EAR

> **Key point**
>
> Your reviewer needs to assess how clearly your key points come across and most importantly whether they help to move the audience in the direction of your objectives.

If you are asked to be 'a critical ear'

If you are asked to review someone else's presentation, meeting plan or document remember that to add real value you need to consider it as though you are the *audience,* not *yourself* and you need to know the *speaker's objectives.*

Without these pre-requisites you will only be able to comment superficially as the only thing you can really check is whether the order is logical. Most senior people will prepare a presentation that is logical, the problem is that what is logical to the speaker isn't necessarily logical to the audience and you need to listen as though you are the audience. So a few tips to help you really add value as a *critical ear:*

- **Think of yourself as the audience** – I find it helpful to think of myself as a caricature of the key person or people. For example, if the audience is a CEO who is known to be strong and autocratic, I imagine myself leaning back in an enormous leather chair, feet on the table, barking out commands.
- **Know what the objectives are** – if you don't understand them, ask for clarification before you begin.
- **Jot down every question or comment that comes to mind** – if it comes into your mind it might come into the audience's.
- **Question as much as you can** – when the presenter

is confidently able to deal with all your questions and comments, you can both be sure that the presentation is sound and well thought through.

At the end of the session you should be able to encourage the other person and boost their confidence.

Making 'getting a critical ear' work for you

Having someone listen with 'a critical ear' is vital, particularly if you are working alone. They bring an outsider's view and whilst they will not be the actual audience, they can certainly help you see how other people might interpret your message.

The key points to remember about Stage 7 are:

- **Use two people as reviewers** – ideally have one who knows the subject and one who doesn't.
- **Leave your ego at home** – I am sure you can work out why.
- **Plan ahead** – Schedule time for the review and making changes. If your first review is two days before the presentation or meeting, there is usually very little that you can change without putting the speaker under so much pressure that you cannot expect a good result.
- **Acknowledge the positive and welcome the negative** – it is great to know what actually works well but it is *vital* to know the things that could be misunderstood, the messages that didn't get across, as well as the things that you didn't intend.
- **Type up your post event review** – use it as a starting point for next time.

No time for 'getting a critical ear'

If you have no time to get someone to review what you have prepared then you are running a significant risk. However, if you have involved other people along the way you might get away with it.

Other ideas that can help you are:

- **Schedule time for reviews at the outset** – as soon as you know that you have an important meeting or presentation to prepare for, schedule some time with your reviewers.
- **Do the review by phone or email if you cannot do it face-to-face** – you need to know the other person very well for this to work as you lose so much non-verbal communication over the telephone.

What next?

At this point you should have a clear and concise piece of communication based on clear objectives and thorough audience research. What you do now will depend on your situation.

For example, you could be going into an informal discussion or a first meeting with a potential client, in which case you probably have all you need to go into that meeting feeling fully prepared.

On the other hand, you might be speaking at a major conference, in which case you will need to spend time crafting your script, polishing your stories and analogies, designing visual aids for the audience, setting memory triggers for yourself and rehearsing your delivery.

Whatever your situation, I recommend that you now have a brief pause in your preparation. If possible give your subconscious a couple of days to mull over what you have done so far.

If you have followed the **Be Clear Seven Stage Process**™ you can rest assured that you have thoroughly prepared the foundation for a great piece of communication.

After that, all it remains for me to say is *Good Luck and Have Fun*!

CASE STUDIES – STAGE 7

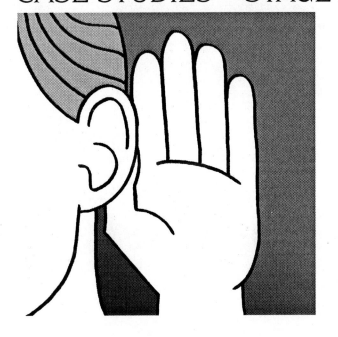

GETTING A CRITICAL EAR

Boffin the Inventor

Working through various stages of the process with Igor and Sally has given Boffin quite a lot of constructive review and challenge. He has been amazed at some of the things that they have told him and suggested. So much so that he has agreed to Sally's recommendation for a final review from one of her colleagues at the marketing company that she works for. Sally recently spent several evenings helping her colleague Debs prepare for an important job interview and she knows that Debs would be delighted to return the favour.

Debs has never met Boffin and knows nothing about the Turbo Powered Wimbley Stick but she does deal with a couple of clients who supply components into the automotive industry. So she should be able to help Boffin refine his message even more.

Peter the Project Manager

Peter and Chris have been working through the process together and they think that they have covered most aspects. However, when Peter was going through Stage 2 – *phoning six friends* he talked to his mate Jerry who runs a similar size department at the local council. To Peter's surprise, Jerry actually offered to provide an external review if Peter thought it would be helpful.

Peter and Jerry found a Saturday afternoon when they were both free and agreed that would be a good time to go through Peter's plan for the meeting. By agreeing the date with Jerry well in advance, Peter had to complete the rest of the process in time, rather than leaving it to the last minute.

After they do the review Peter and Chris are taking Jerry to his favourite restaurant as a 'thank you'.

Chrystal and Christof the Creativity Consultants

In effect Mike's work with Chrystal and Christof has been their final review. They really do not have time to involve anyone else at this stage.

However, for the future they have all agreed that as soon as they know the date they will be having an important meeting or presentation they will immediately put a date in the diary for a review meeting several days ahead. They will also think of who else they need to involve in the process and at what point.

In fact Chrystal and Christof will never prepare anything in such isolation again. They know the importance of involving other people to develop creative solutions, they had just never really applied it to new business proposals before . . . a bit like the cobbler who never mends his shoes!

APPENDICES

Appendix 1 –
How a message
can change

The words I would use to describe my journey to work if my objective is to make you **think** that you have been informed about my journey:

I left home this morning at about 7.00am. I drove my car along a series of unclassified roads until I came to the junction with the main road from Lutterworth to Leicester. I turned left to join the main road and drove for about 12 miles towards Leicester. Once I got into the city I took a series of turns to take me to the south east side of the city and arrived at my office at 7.28am.

The words I would use to describe my journey to work if my objective is to make you **feel** inspired about my journey:

I live in a small village near Lutterworth and as I left home at about 7 o'clock this morning the birds were singing and the sun was shining. It really was a glorious morning. I whizzed along the country lanes for a couple of miles and then joined the main road into Leicester. It's a really fun road to drive with very little to slow you down until you get well into the city. This morning was a particularly clear drive even when I got into the centre, so I was parked outside my office within half an hour feeling fit and ready to start the day.

Appendix 2 –
Emotions

Some of the common emotions that you might want the audience to **feel** during parts of your communication are:

Alarmed

Awed

Calm

Comfortable

Concerned

Confident

Curious

Disappointed

Enlivened

Excited

Fascinated

Frightened

Frustrated

Happy

Inquisitive

Inspired

Interested

Intrigued

Involved

Optimistic

Passionate

Relaxed

Surprised

Threatened

Uneasy

Do bear in mind that if you take people into a negative emotion, you will probably need to move them to a more positive one by the end of your time with them, so use negative emotions with care.

Appendix 3 –
Questions,
questions

Some questions that are useful to consider when researching your audience are:

Who is the audience?

What type of person / people are they?

Will they want us to be direct, or will they want to have a long preamble?

What power or influence do they have?

How will we be communicating?

What is the demographic profile?

What is their educational background?

What do they love / hate?

How should I structure the message?

Are they pro or anti our cause?

What do they know about the subject?

What do they know about me / us?

Will they understand the terminology?

What else will they be thinking about?

How does this fit with their other priorities?

How likely are they to go off at a tangent?

When will they receive the communication?

What style / tone will they prefer?

What will their pre-conceptions be?

What are they expecting?

Who else might be at the meeting / reading the document?

Will they all have the same background?

What do they need to know?

What extra information should I include?

What are their 'hot buttons'?

What will help them to gain politically?

How can we make this supportive to them?

How do we let them know what to expect?

Who else knows the audience?

For a conference / seminar what else do I need to know?

Always ask yourself – what matters to the audience?

Appendix 4 –
Introductions

Your introduction must grab the audience's attention whilst also adding to your message. If you are not particularly confident as a presenter, use something like a question or a quotation. If you are more confident, let your imagination and creativity come up with something really memorable!

- **Use a quotation or relevant fact** – this is a relatively low risk approach, however, your audience will be flattered that you are well prepared and they will have something to engage them.

- **Ask the audience a question** – then pause to give them a chance to think about the question, but be prepared, they may even answer you!

- **Make a contentious statement** – saying something that the audience will disagree with or feel threatened by is comparatively high risk, but can be very effective.

- **Tell an 'everyday' story that the audience can relate to** – remember even if a lot of the audience know your subject, they will be impressed if you can make a complex subject easy to understand.

- **Get the audience to discover something themselves** – people remember things that they learn for themselves, even if it is something quite simple.

- **Use a prop or do something unusual** – this will work as long as it relates strongly to your subject matter, but beware, tricks and gimmicks are rarely forgiven by an audience.

- **Link to a previous presentation** – a strong image or sound from a previous presentation will immediately provide context for your talk.

Appendix 5 – Reviewers questions

Objectives	• Do they make sense?
	• Are they consistent?
Audience profile	• Could / should we know more?
	• Who else could we ask?
	• What are the audience expecting?
Content	• Does it make you **think, feel, say** and **do** the objectives?
	• What else do you **think, feel, say** and **do**?
	• What are the key messages?
	• Is there anything that can be taken out?
	• Is there anything else to include?
Structure	• Is the structure clear – 3, 5 or lots?
	• Is it the correct structure for this particular audience?
Signposting	• Is the level of signposting right for the audience?
	• Will it help the audience re-engage?
Overall	• Are we using 'house style' for terms?
	• Are we slipping into jargon?
	• Is the language / tone appropriate?
	• How could the communication be improved / made easier for the audience to understand?
	• Are the introduction and conclusion clear and concise, including the 'call to action'?

Appendix 6 –
Post event
review

Complete this review to help you maximise your learnings from this piece of communication and enable you to build on them for the future.

Review of _____ on _____ 20xx	
Did the audience **think, feel, say** and **do** what we wanted them to **think, feel, say** and **do** – what evidence was there?	
What went well?	
What didn't go well or as planned?	
What could we possibly have done differently?	

BIBLIOGRAPHY

Bowman, Lee *High Impact Presentations* Bene Factum
Publishing Ltd
ISBN: 0952275457

Buzan, Tony & Barry *The Mind Map Book: Radiant
Thinking - Major Evolution in Human Thought* BBC Books
ISBN: 0563487011

The Economist *Style Guide* Economist Books
ISBN: 1861972091

Lewis, Harold *Bids, Tenders & Proposals* Kogan Page
ISBN: 0749443693

Minto, Barbara *The Pyramid Principle* Financial Times
Prentice Hall
ISBN: 0273659030

Rouse & Rouse *Business Communications, A Cultural and
Strategic Approach* Thomson Learning
ISBN: 1861525443

Stanton, Nicky *Mastering Communication* Palgrave
Macmillan
ISBN: 1403917094

Stuart, Christina *Effective Speaking* Gower
ISBN: 0-566-02803-4

ABOUT THE AUTHOR

Christine Searancke assists senior executives with clear, concise and outstanding communications.

During her 17 years in the Financial Services Sector, she gained broad management experience before working on a major transformation project alongside a 'Top 5' management consultancy. Ultimately she was responsible for the content of all presentations and documents submitted to the Board and external partners.

In 2000 she established her own consultancy, Be Clear Ltd. She now helps business and professional people from all sectors to write compelling presentations and proposals, as well as working with them to thoroughly prepare for meetings and workshops. Over the years she has developed and refined the tools and techniques in this book. Witnessing their success time and time again she knows they work. In addition, Christine runs focused workshops where experienced presenters have the opportunity to discover these tools and take their own communication skills to new levels.

Christine can be contacted at christine@beclear.co.uk or +44(0)845 456 7094. Or go to www.beclear.co.uk.

WHAT PEOPLE ARE SAYING

"Christine Searancke provides insight into the make or break presentation, pitch or other opportunity for business communication. She identifies common sense approaches to researching your audience, deciding how to achieve the result you desire and the value of practice and review."

Andy Gilgrist, Business Editor, Leicester Mercury

"Helps you realise that the presentation is about your audience, not about you."

Jonathan Flowers, Deputy Chief Executive, Bedfordshire County Council

"If you often have too much material for a presentation and are reluctant to cut, you really need this book. The simple techniques helped me to greatly reduce preparation time and influence my audience to more effectively achieve my objectives."

Chris Roberts, General Manager, Business Customer Satisfaction & Service, BT Business

"The way it makes you focus on objectives is really powerful. I use the process in meetings and emails as well as presentations – in fact I use it whenever I'm communicating!"

Selwyn Herring, Chief Executive Officer, Synaptic Systems Ltd

"We used the ideas in this book when preparing for a pitch for business - and they helped us to win a contract with one of the UK's top local authorities!"

Tony Barradell, Director, Insight People Development Ltd

"It is often a daunting task to prepare and deliver a formal presentation only then to find out that the audience have gone away with mixed messages. This book provides a very clear process and some excellent but simple techniques that when used will ensure that the audience will go away with a very clear understanding of your message."

Chris Rowland, Credit Manager, HSBC Bank plc

"An excellent book, it helps you do exactly 'what it says on the tin'."

David Allcock, Managing Partner, Rowley's Accountants

"If communication and influence are an important part of your work, this book is not only a 'must read', but also a really handy ongoing reference tool. I liked the practical structure and examples, which really brought the subject to life."

Andy Towse, Senior Development Manager, Barclays

Printed in the United Kingdom
by Lightning Source UK Ltd.
109651UKS00002B/1